WITH THEIR EARS
PRICKED FORWARD

JOHN F. BLAIR, PUBLISHER
Winston-Salem, North Carolina

JOHN F. BLAIR, PUBLISHER
Winston-Salem, North Carolina

WITH THEIR EARS PRICKED FORWARD

TALES OF MULES I'VE KNOWN

Joshua A. Lee

Library of Congress Catalog Card Number 80–19667
Printed in the United States of America
by Heritage Printers, Inc., Charlotte, North Carolina

Second Printing, 1981

Library of Congress Cataloging in Publication Data

Lee, Joshua A   1924–
    With their ears pricked forward.

    1. Mules–Legends and stories.   I. Title.
SF362.L43   636.1'8   80–19667
ISBN 0–89587–018–5

To my father, Carson Lee
A pretty good mule man himself

CONTENTS

WITH THEIR EARS
PRICKED FORWARD

MEN WHO KNEW MULES

MY DADDY was a mule man, as was his father before him. By that I mean they found pleasure in owning lots of mules, liked to buy and sell them, and favored their company when feeling down and out. I grew up in the Upper Coastal Plain of Georgia near Millerville, a little town just south of the red Piedmont and a couple of rivers over from South Carolina. When I was a boy, the humble mule was the chief source of tractive power on the local farms, and across the entire South for that matter. Folks claimed that mules were steadier than horses and had more gumption about farm work. They were certainly a lot more nimble of foot around tender cotton plants, and they stood the fierce summer heat better. Therefore the welfare of a farm family depended upon the stamina and quality of its workstock.

My grandfather, Old Cap'n Tolbert to the local black folks, was a county commissioner off and on and served a term or two in the state legislature, but he was best known as a planter. In his heyday, between about 1890 and 1930, the Old Cap'n ran about fifty plows and spent much time picking mules for his own operations, and for his neighbors and the local mule merchants. Thus he was known far and wide as a shrewd judge of muleflesh, and much status accrued from that gift. A mule was a pretty fair investment for a farmer in those days—a good pair sold for as high as $300—so mistakes in sizing up a new purchase could push a man and his family that much closer to the margin of despair. Therefore people were grateful for Grandfather's help and advice when they were in the market for a new mule, so much so, in fact, that often when he left for the big mule sales in Atlanta and Chattanooga, he took along orders for as many as a hundred head.

Grandfather insisted that there wasn't all that much to picking mules. All it took was a little common sense, some experience, and a lot of patience. The Old Cap'n was known for understating his position in the community. His modesty was that of a confident man, one who could accomplish more accidentally than most could on purpose. Casual though he might have seemed, he must have cut a formidable figure as he prowled the auction barns, a tall, spare figure with white handlebar moustache and intense blue eyes, ever on the alert for likely mules to buy.

Typically a mule at the big sales moved through an auction ring, but shrewd buyers like Old Cap'n Tolbert had no time for that kind of marketing. He argued that the only function of an auctioneer was to talk dollars onto a mule's price tag. Instead of bidding against people who he claimed didn't know the difference between a decent mule and a brindled ox, Grandfather roamed the stalls, picking out likely-looking mules and arranging private sales.

Grandfather's routine for testing a new mule was simple and straightforward. He'd enter a stable quietly and flip his hat at the occupant. If the mule snorted and cringed against the stable wall, Grandfather moved on to the next stall. Mules that get rattled when challenged are apt to be foolish and flighty if not downright dangerous to be around.

If a mule didn't respond to the hat flip, Grandfather might judge it to be hardheaded or too no-account and slow to turn out a good day's work. However, there were many good mules that were just naturally easygoing. Grandfather often tested a slow-acting mule by rubbing it along the belly. If a mule came alert and didn't flinch when its belly was rubbed, Grandfather judged it to be an animal with some energy and considered it further.

Astute buyers agreed that a quality mule should stand firm and not show alarm when tested, though it should perk up and act alive. Such mules might stare a prospective buyer in the face in a knowing sort of way, but that was not necessarily bad. Some people believed that bold-acting mules were potential troublemakers, but Grandfather believed that boldness denoted intelligence. Blinders were used routinely on horses and mules, and those usually curbed any tendency for a mule to be curious about what its driver was up to.

Most planters liked stylish mules, the kind that stood tall and looked proud. Old Cap'n Tolbert rarely bought a mule that was sway-backed, or ewe-necked, or one whose ears flopped back and forth when it walked. Such mules might step well to a single-stock plow, but they never looked good in an important planter's cotton field. It was as important to Grandfather that a mule look right as it was for the jarhead to work right. Still, I'd be telling less than the truth if I claimed that the Old Cap'n never deviated from his notions about style in mules. Old Carrie, a smallish, dun-colored mule, was his all-time favorite, and she resembled a donkey about as much as she did a mule. She was real swift to a plow, and she was tireless. Grandfather told me once that she teamed up with one Prince Henry Jackson and sided nearly six acres of cotton in a day's time, a record that still stands in Ogeechee County. And of course folks around home remember that Grandfather brought Old Alec into our country. That old humpbacked jarhead's contrariness became a legend as far as two counties over.

Farmers in the Upper Plain liked good-sized mules but didn't want them too big, a half-ton to fourteen hundred pounds being about right. That size mule was commonly called a cotton mule, a class bred mostly in the dolomitic hills and basins of Tennessee and Kentucky. Mustang, or peewee, mules, bred mostly in Texas, were usually too lightweight for most classes of farm work, and Grandfather and his cohorts were willing to leave the large draft types, bred mostly in Missouri, to loggers.

Mated mules, teams trained to work together, were greatly prized, and Grandfather was always on the lookout for them. Sometimes mated mules were matched—that is, they were the same sex and color, and the same, or near the same, age. Planters agreed that it was always best to keep mated teams intact because mules, like people, develop strong attachments and seem happiest when living and working together. Grandfather owned several pairs of mates during the many years he farmed and bought mules, and I remember a few pairs that my father owned.

Most mules, like people, have a definite hand, or perhaps more properly foot, preference. In double harness each member of a team likes to work with its favored hoof to the inside. Hitch a team up wrong and they're likely to crowd the tongue, or pull outward instead of straight ahead, or even try to run away. A mule of Daddy's named Alice would actually step over a wagon tongue to get to the side she preferred.

When sizing up a new mule, it was therefore important to know which hoof it favored. Grandfather judged a mule's hoof preference by walking the animal for a short distance. If not startled, a mule will practically always lift its natural hoof first. Another way to tell is to lead a mule out of its stable. After a short pause at the door, a mule lifts its preferred hoof first and places it carefully over the doorsill. Very likely a jarhead will stomp you with its favored hoof, if it's that kind of mule. Neither the Old Cap'n nor anyone else I ever knew recommended that as a way to find out about a mule's hoof preference.

Some horses and mules get dizzy and stagger about after being made to travel continuously in a circle, as when pulling the sweep of a cane-grinding mill. Mr. Dawse Cook, the local blacksmith, claimed that a mule got dizzy going around in a circle if it couldn't rotate with its natural hoof to the inside. Although Mr. Cook's explanation always seemed plausible to me, Grandfather didn't necessarily go along with it. He claimed that some mules, like a few people he knew, were just naturally inclined to be dizzy in the head. Be that as it may, if one blindfolds a dizzy mule, it can circle without further trouble. However, it is not wise to tamper with the vision of a mule you don't know well. Trying to blindfold a nervous, skitterish mule is a quick way to get maimed.

Grandfather, as well as my own father and most other planters around home, preferred mare mules, or jennies, for farm work because they were alleged to be steadier and stepped out better than horse mules, or jacks. Horse mules, however, were more powerful on the average than mare mules. In fact, few mare mules could match the strength of horse mules of the same weight. With rare exception horse mules were more peaceable among themselves than mare mules. That was because mare mules invariably established a rigid peck order when two or more were penned up together, and that led to intermittent strife.

Even though the Old Cap'n professed to prefer mare mules, some of the best and most fondly remembered jarheads in his stables were horse mules—mules like Bob Senior and Bob Junior and Old Alec, who lived on to vex my father for many years after Grandfather's passing. The main reason that planters were leery of horse mules was that many of them developed bad habits as their lives wore on. Sometimes those quirks could be dangerous, as with Rox, a tough outlaw mule who once belonged to my uncle Lester Tolbert. Fortunately most of the eccentricities of horse mules were of the merely aggravating kind. For example, our neighbor, Mr. Clay Parker, once owned a mule named Dirty Red, who wouldn't cross a plank bridge unless enough dirt had been heaped over it to muffle his hoof-beats. Sometimes wrapping his hooves in croaker sacks would work.

Mules, like all farm animals, had their illnesses, and during the cotton days of my boyhood, planters spent much time doctoring sick workstock, or else arguing over the best remedy for glanders, or swinny, or this malady or that. Although most of the treatments were based solely upon lore and superstition, they often worked, or perhaps the animals' complaints were just naturally of the self-limiting kind. The formal practice of veterinary medicine was something of a novelty at the time, and many planters were downright leery of such highfalutin notions as preventive vaccination, the use of serums, and odd-looking pills in tinted bottles.

Although Grandfather was a pretty good mule doctor in his own right, he and his neighbors relied mostly upon a black citizen named Swint Fuller when their stock needed veterinary attention. Old Swint plied his trade on an itinerant basis, and although the man had no formal training in veterinary science, he was a veritable wizard at divining the ills of farm animals. Old Doc Swint was an authority on the treatment of swint, or swinny, a kind of lameness in a mule's withers or shoulders. Some claimed that he'd come by his nickname in that way. He was also an expert at treating cramp colic, gravel (a kind of mule constipation), and founder, or lamination. He floated teeth and gave advice on feeding and mineral nutrition. I remember that he recommended a kind of mineral block called Dr. Blackburn's Lick-a-Brick as a spring tonic. Once Daddy had a couple of mules who were addicted to eating dirt, and Dr. Fuller advised him to keep a billy goat in the barn lot. Presumably the goat would stink up the premises so bad that the mules wouldn't want to eat the dirt. One of our mules, Old Lou, stomped the poor old billy to death, and that ended our experiment with goats.

Windbreak, or bellows, was an all-too-common misery among horses and mules in the old days. The malady seemed something like asthma, or perhaps emphysema, in humans. A bellowsed mule coughed after the slightest exertion and couldn't perform even the easiest work. Swint Fuller laid much of the windbreak in local stock to the consumption of moldy corn fodder. Curiously, Grandfather had come to the same conclusion more than a year before.

Old Cap'n Tolbert passed on in 1936 at the age of sixty-five—not a particularly long life by modern standards but a full one nonetheless. At the time, the mule was still about the only practical source of draft power on Southern farms, but that was to change in a few short years. Although Grandfather had the reputation of being an innovator in his time, a man quick to see the potential in new ways, I don't believe he would have been pleasured any having to live on a farm worked by tractors. I say that because, with the Old Cap'n, owning mules and watching them work was much more than a matter of simple utility; it was an emotionally rewarding way of life.

Daddy told me once that when Grandfather felt the press of responsibilities more than usual, he liked to go down to the

7

barn lot and curry and pet his buggy horse and any mules that happened to be idle. When the Old Cap'n felt that way, others gave him a wide berth. Most didn't care to test his temper, but beyond that, all knew that he needed the comfort of associating with sentient brutes who couldn't run their mouths and make demands upon him.

Thus Old Cap'n Tolbert, like his neighbors, made pets of his workstock. My daddy tended to be that way too, but perhaps to a lesser degree than his father. Likely Daddy's way presaged the change that was inevitable—the replacement of the humble mule with the powerful, though unfeeling, farm tractor. I don't think the Old Cap'n would have gotten much satisfaction out of petting a six-row tractor rig.

DOWN TO THE BRIDLE

MOST of the people I knew during my earlier years were dirt poor—so poor, in fact, that for many of them merely fending off the wolf was a daily adventure. I've heard grown men claim that they'd forgotten whose picture was on a five-dollar bill, and others who couldn't remember what store-boughten groceries tasted like. Not overly prosperous to begin with, the Upper Plain practically ground to a halt when cotton fell to a nickel a pound during the Great Depression. Some said that it was like pioneer days all over again. People had to return to growing practically everything they ate and bartering among themselves for whatever else they might need.

My set, the planter and merchant class, were somewhat better off than most, and there was, of course, the pride of ancestry. Perhaps the latter was the main reason "proper" folks looked down upon the likes of Frank Sugg. Frank, like most others, was of obscure background and his schooling was meager, but the man never accepted his lot the way others in the same straits were inclined to do. Instead, he tried hard to educate himself by reading everything he could lay hands on and to absorb refinement by hobnobbing with those he regarded as the upper crust. Unfortunately, Frank's reading skills were only marginal to begin with, and his frame of reference for relating new knowledge to previous experience was shaky at best, so much on the printed pages only confused him or else eluded his grasp. As a consequence, poor Frank bewildered the semiliterate with his big words while at the same time earning the contempt of those he wished to impress.

Most pathetic of all was when Frank came to church on Sundays and tried to throw his weight around. He prayed and sang louder than anybody else in the congregation and seized upon the barest of excuses to step forward and confess his own sins and the sins of others. It was a caution the way he kept Fent Newsome and his retailers on the griddle by divulging the ins and outs of their moonshining operations before Deacon Josh Wiggins and the other high churchmen. Frank naturally had strong opinions about all things pertaining to religion and tried hard to impress the deacons and trustees that he was the man to help them run the church. But whereas those dignitaries were willing enough to lend an ear to any town dirt Frank might dredge up, they spurned his advice on matters of policy and protocol.

Frank's antics sorely vexed Reverend Theodore Martin, our red-haired preacher. Reverend Martin had his hands full mollifying the clique that paid his salary while attempting at the same time to foster the image of the church as a community open to all, and Frank's pushy ways didn't help matters one bit. Still, caught as he was between the upper and nether stones of exclusion by one group and rejection by another, Frank displayed a good spirit, and that evoked the sympathies of some few folks, including Daddy and the Old Cap'n, who believed that the man was a cut above average.

Frank's big chance came in 1935, or so it appeared at the time. Among the many welfare programs of the depression years was a kind of agricultural resettlement for the poverty-stricken. Citizens judged poor enough, yet potentially capable, were allowed to settle on rented land with the option to buy the acreage should they prove successful in establishing themselves as farmers. The settlers were supplied with workstock, farm implements, and credit to get started, along with free government food. The recipients of all that public largess were under the supervision of an appropriate bureau, and the rules governing the disposal of granted properties were alleged to be strict.

The Burleson estate was under probate at the time, the elder Mr. Burleson having passed on in 1933. The resettlement bureau rented a tract from the heirs and divided it into sixty-acre parcels for distribution to qualified settlers. With Grandfather standing as character witness, Frank Sugg applied for a homestead, and his application was among the first approved.

Frank received a fine pair of mules named Kate and Docey as part of his stake. Grandfather had bought the mules earlier for consignment to Parker's Stables. On getting the news that Frank had picked the best pair of mules available to work his new farm, Grandfather got in his buggy and drove to Millerville to offer his congratulations. The Old Cap'n cautioned Frank to take good care of his mules and see to it that they were fed regularly. Frank assured Grandfather that Kate and Docey would get the best of care, and that done, he drove his new team home to start a crop.

All went well at first. Frank tended his crop regularly and kept his fields real clean until about the first of June. Then the Ogeechee River began to fall, and the fish started biting. Frank took to spending more and more time on the river while the grass gained on his crop. By the Fourth of July crab grass and cockleburs had his cotton and corn by the throat, so that he couldn't have plowed them clean even if he had tried. As a result there was little if any crop to be gathered when fall rolled around.

By November Frank's supply of government feed had run

out, and Kate and Docey got thin. Frank looked them over and decided that he didn't need such a big, strapping pair of mules to tend his few piddling acres. They ate too blamed much anyway. He swapped them to a farmer over in Buford County for a pair of smallish plugs named Sam and Cracker, and got a hundred bushels of corn to boot. The logical thing for Frank to do was to feed the corn to his new mules to keep them in shape for the spring plowing. Tooky Calhoun told it around that Frank swapped most of the corn to Fent Newsome for moonshine.

Sam and Cracker had to eat, so Frank turned them out to forage as best they could in his weed-grown fields. After the mules had nibbled away all the frosted grass available, Frank took to stealing for them—a bundle of fodder here, a block of peavine hay there, and a few ears of corn over yonder. Daddy told me that more than once he'd spied Frank sneaking into our barn after dark to get feed for his mules. Daddy felt so sorry for the poor animals, if not for Frank himself, that he pretended not to notice. Evidently there were others in the community who felt the same way.

When spring came, Sam and Cracker were in fair shape for starting a crop, but Frank decided that he didn't need a team to work his little one-horse farm. At the time there was a Gypsy caravan camped on the edge of town, so Frank took his team down to see what the Romanies would offer him in exchange. Those swarthy traders must have been happy to see the likes of Frank. Gypsies had the reputation in those days of being a sharp bunch to deal with. They were notorious for training trick horses and mules to vex gullible buyers once the Gypsies had left town. The hapless buyer was usually more than glad to unload the seemingly demented animal on the next caravan that happened through, and virtually always at a substantial loss. Grandfather claimed that the second Gypsy band always worked in cahoots with the first.

When Frank accepted a two-for-one swap, that particular troop probably saw little point in sticking him with a trick mule. Frank's new mule, named Ellabelle, was a flat-mouthed twelve-year-old, and proved to be a right handy mule as long as Frank stole enough feed to keep her going. Then the fish started biting and Frank stopped tending his crop and stealing feed, both. Poor Old Ellabelle wasted away on crabgrass, as had Sam and Cracker before her, so that by the end of summer she was practically down on the lift.

About that time Frank began to dream of owning a horse. A horse can be worked through the week like a mule, but is much more fashionable to ride to town on Saturdays. Frank found a horse that suited his tastes at a stable in Jenkins County, and must have been mighty surprised when the owner offered to swap his animal for Ellabelle without asking for any boot.

Frank's new horse was a striking blood-bay. It couldn't have been more than eight years old and had plenty of spirit. Frank leaked it around that he had a fine steed and deliberately stayed away from town that Saturday in order to whet the local appetite for a view of his new charge. When Grandfather heard about Frank's sharp deal, he just shook his head and sighed. He felt that there had to be something bad the matter with the horse. It probably had the start of a bad case of the glanders, or was bellowsed, or worse.

Frank picked a bright Saturday afternoon in August for his triumphant entry. The horse sidled and pranced along Main Street while the crowd gawked. Frank grinned like a shoat in hog heaven.

Frank reined his mount up in front of the post office and sat beaming while the crowd gathered around to admire the bay.

A short way off, Sam Catoe and some of his cronies stood slouching against the front of Evans' General Store. Old Sam winked at no one in particular, nudged Foots Mathis in the ribs, and yelled out: "Hey, Frank! They tell me that plug of yours can't outrun Fent Newsome's Old Pender Jane."

Frank swung around and glared at Sam in annoyance. "Whoever told you that ain't got no more sense than a mud turkle. Hell, this horse can outrun anything on four legs this side of the Ogeechee River."

With that Frank pumped his knees and the horse took off in a gallop. Four or five of us kids tried to keep up, but we were left behind in a cloud of dust before Frank turned the corner at the blacksmith shop. I raced back to the post office and arrived just as Frank's horse sprinted around Evans' store and headed back up Main Street. About ten strides from the post office, the bay pulled up and started heaving. Frank barely had time enough to slide off the stricken horse's back before it collapsed and gave up the ghost in the middle of the street.

The crowd stood in stunned silence. No one seemed to be able to move or even speak until Sam Catoe nodded sheepishly to Frank and slunk away. Then people drifted off one by one, leaving Frank holding the dead horse's reins. All Frank Sugg had to show for his trading was a bridle.

When word of Frank's misfortune finally got back to the resettlement office, the area director decided, belatedly, that all of Frank's dealings had been contrary to the rules after all. There were rumors that Frank would be prosecuted for fraud, but other than his being summarily evicted from the resettlement tract, nothing startling came of the matter. Deacon Josh Wiggins, who believed that all of Mr. Roosevelt's programs were designed to make sorry people even sorrier, claimed that the government had gone easy on Frank because the local agent had been afraid that the big boys up the line would land on him if he didn't keep the lid on in his sector.

Somehow Frank managed to keep body and soul together until World War II brought better times. Then, taking advantage of the increased demand for labor, Frank hired on with the Central Railroad as a maintenance man looking after right-of-way properties. Good wages and the settled routine of steady employment did wonders for Frank. He became a solid citizen, and with his new status came the respect from others that he craved so much. When I got home from the army in 1946, Frank was a deacon in the First Baptist Church, and he frequently led the congregation in prayer. He still used a fifty-cent word now and then, but folks can overlook such behavior in a man who pays his bills regularly.

A couple of summers back Daddy and I were standing by the artesian well in the town square when I heard a spirited clip-clopping approaching from up the street. I turned and beheld Frank Sugg sitting a handsome palomino. Mr. Sugg wore spangled western regalia, and his mount was decked out in a splendid saddle and a silver-studded bridle. Frank greeted Daddy warmly and tossed me an offhand nod as if he'd taken me for a stranger. That was not surprising since I hadn't seen Frank in nearly twenty years. Later Daddy told me that Frank had recently retired from the railroad and held investments in farm lands and timber. Right then and there I had a feeling that Mr. Frank Sugg would never be down to the bridle again.

MARY, A BOSS MULE

HORSES and their relatives normally live in small herds, and when animals dwell in groups, interactions among the members of the band follow in due course. Within a given herd a social hierarchy develops, that is to say, a peck order. Some individuals take over as leaders, whereas others assume subordinate roles.

Among wild horses a social unit consists of a mature stallion accompanied by upwards of a dozen mares. Although the internal affairs of the stud's harem are governed by the mares, the stallion is in his turn a despot over all. A wild stud will brook no sass from his charges, and will fight virtually to the death to repel any rival that tries to depose him.

The social order of the donkey, the other side of the mule's family, is very different. Mature jacks choose not to live full time with jennies, preferring instead to dwell in territories of their own choosing. Jennies, on the other hand, band together in small herds, each led by an experienced member. Like wild stallions, boss jennies exercise total authority over their herd mates.

During the mating season a territorial jack seeks out a herd of jennies and remains until their amatory needs are fulfilled. Then, doubtless satisfied that he has performed his duties to the best of his abilities, the weary jackass retires to enjoy once more the relative tranquillity of his chosen domain.

Mules do not, of course, exist in the wild, so there is no way of knowing how they might order their societies in the harsh realm of fang and claw. However, there is information, albeit sketchy, on the ways mules shape their hierarchies in the domesticated state, and there they seem to favor the donkey type of organization over that of the horse.

Within a given barn lot a mare mule will invariably be the boss, with the other mules ranked in slots below her. I've seen a great many mare mules exercising their prerogatives as bosses, and have on a few occasions watched mules fight to see who would wind up as boss. Mules, like horses and asses, fight with their heels and teeth. They slash and kick, and jostle and bite. Once rank has been sorted out, the winner enforces her position with threatening gestures, the most common being a thrust of the head at the rival, usually with the ears laid back and the teeth bared. This gesture is often accompanied by a loud, throaty hum. Again like horses and donkeys, mules squeal and hum when they fight, the volume rising and falling with the pace of the action.

Horse mules rarely participate in the shaping of the peck order, remaining, as it were, mostly on the fringes of the herd. In fact, I never saw a horse mule involved in a struggle for dominance. Perhaps that's because male equines do not normally fight with females. But the fact that horse mules rarely fight among themselves leads me to believe that they haven't any desire to do battle in the first place. All horse mules I ever saw were geldings; thus robbed of status, they might well have lost whatever will to command they had in the first place.

It's hard to typify the personality of a boss mule except to note that she's bossy with other mules. The difficulty is compounded when one realizes that within a given herd a mule might outrank several others, yet still not be boss. Therefore, a jarhead might be the leader in one barn lot and rank well down the hierarchy in the next. In some herds, particularly large ones, command is likely to shift from time to time, so being boss is frequently related not only to a mule's personality, but to place and circumstance as well.

Some boss mules I've known were steady and easygoing, like Old Ada, who was not only the boss of the barn lot at the Burke Lumber Company during the 1930s but also the leader of a crack timber-cart span. Other boss mules of my acquaintance were ill-tempered brutes who were apt to be as bossy with their owners as with other mules. Old Mary, a mule my daddy bought from a band of Romany Gypsies, was typical of the cantankerous kind of boss mule.

We acquired Mary one Saturday afternoon in late September of 1935. I'd been walking to school the Friday morning before, and not being overly anxious to get to my classes, I'd stopped to listen to the jizzywits rasping away in the dog fennels that lined the public road. I'd dawdled for perhaps five minutes when I heard laughter and the tinkling sounds of little bells. I looked up and beheld a Gypsy caravan rounding a bend and heading straight toward me. I was alarmed at first but calmed down when the old chieftain at the head of the train reined up, smiled unctuously, and asked if my father was at home. I pointed in the direction of our house. The old Gypsy thanked me and rode on, followed by a procession of wagons, work stock, and goats.

When I got home from school that afternoon, the Gypsies were camped in a hayfield across the road from our house. Unlike Grandfather, Daddy was fascinated by Gypsies and never passed up a chance to trade with them. The Old Cap'n wouldn't allow Gypsies on his premises. He felt that the swarthy rogues, as he called them, were so slick they could steal the corns off your toes without so much as ruffling your socks. It was obvious that the Gypsy chieftain had talked

Daddy into putting the caravan up for the night, and that there would be trading in the morning. I noted that several of the Gypsy horses and mules were busily nibbling our haystacks, but no one, including Daddy, seemed to mind.

Near dusk the Gypsy women started cook fires, and before long the aroma of a savory stew drifted in on the evening breeze, making me a little hungrier than usual and prompting our old dog, Driver, to howl in anticipation of her overdue supper. After the evening meal the Gypsy camp came alive with music and dancing, drawing us kids like a magnet. Unlike Daddy, Mama didn't trust Gypsies, having heard that they would kidnap untended children. We'd no sooner settled down to enjoy the festivities than she rounded us up and sent us off to bed a full hour earlier than we were accustomed to going. Naturally we climbed out the bedroom window and sneaked back over to the camp.

Those Romanies were a delight to watch. They never seemed to tire of dancing and playing what sounded to me like the same tune over and over on a violin, two guitars, and a tambourine. The merrymaking was still going strong when my brother and I crept back to bed at 1:00 A.M. The next morning Ceroy Tolbert told me that he'd stayed up and watched them until daybreak.

Some of those Gypsies might not have had any sleep that night, but even so, the menfolks were ready to conduct business the next morning. The old chieftain paraded the Gypsy string before Daddy, Uncle Lester Tolbert, and a few of the neighbors, extolling the virtues of each decrepit plug in turn. Uncle Lester bought a pinto horse, and Mr. Pete Kiner bargained for a mule at what he considered a good price. Daddy didn't see any stock that interested him until he spied a mule tethered behind a tent. The mule looked young and had a proud bearing, although there was hardly enough flesh on her bones to hold them together. The Gypsies didn't seem to want to part with Mary, as they called the mule, but after a prolonged siege of haggling, Daddy finally persuaded them to part with her for twenty-five dollars and twenty bales of peavine hay.

The Gypsy caravan was hardly out of sight before Daddy began to have misgivings about his new purchase. Poor Mary was so perished out and weak she had to walk spraddle-legged to maintain her balance. When Deacon Andrew Tolbert came by to look at her late that afternoon, he declared that he could hang his hat on her off hipbone while his wife Lacey scrubbed out a wash on her ribs.

At the time, we despaired that Mary would ever mend, but she turned out to be a lot tougher than we had thought. On plenty of hay and oats she fleshed out rapidly, and as she regained her strength she got right feisty. One morning in late October she chose out Old Lou, a big bay mule who'd been boss of the barn lot for years. The two fought off and on for days while the other mules cowered in the background. Once when the pair was engaged in a particularly savage round, Mama begged Daddy to separate them before one of them was killed. Daddy just smiled and pointed out that as long as the two were going to have to live together in the same barn lot, they were bound to fight it out sooner or later, and the sooner the better. Mary, through sheer pluck and determination, won, besting a bigger mule on the defendant's home ground. Once she'd secured the position of top mule, all she had to do to enforce her status was lay back her ears and bare her teeth.

Daddy watched Mary take over and decided that if she was strong enough to fight, she was able to go to work. That settled, he took a bridle and went into the lot to catch out the new boss and put her to a plow. Mary took exception to her new owner's rash decision. In fact, she got right nasty, making it plain that she could be dangerous if aroused. She wound up running Daddy out of the lot, and might have injured him badly or even killed him if he hadn't streaked for the gate when she came at him with her hooves a-flailing. As it was, she kicked three planks off the barn-lot gate with a blow that had been meant for my father's head.

Ordinarily Daddy didn't swear around us children, but that morning he broke precedent, declaring among other things that never before in his born days had he taken anything off a damned mule, and that he wasn't about to start with Mary. If the business end of a three-tined hayfork wouldn't cool the hellion down, he'd see how she favored a taste of double-aught buckshot.

When Daddy stepped into the barn lot the second time, he was armed and ready. Mary came out snorting and kicking as before, but Daddy stood his ground. The more she kicked, the more he jabbed her rump with that pitchfork, and that settled her down in a quick hurry.

Judging from her looks after the forking, Mary was more startled than hurt. She gave Daddy a surprised look, clamped her tail down tight, and bucked away into a fence corner, where she stood trembling and subdued. When Daddy approached her for the third time, she thrust her head into the bridle and gave no further trouble.

Deacon Andrew Tolbert worked Mary in double harness with Lou that day, breaking ground for winter oats. That night he reported that Mary was a good steady mule, not overly fast but obedient, and wise to the ways of farm work. Never during the years that Deacon Tolbert worked her did Mary bow-up to him, and rarely did he have to speak to her harshly or discipline her in any way.

Mary continued to try Daddy out from time to time, and she would kick in harness if a person she didn't know or respect got too close to her heels. Some of the plow hands were never able to work her. I remember a Saturday morning when C. T. Tolbert, the Deacon's older son, tried to catch Mary out to haul some firewood. Mary bullyragged the youth until he retreated to a fence corner. Luckily Deacon Tolbert showed up, for Mary was just getting ready to kick his son's brains out. Not surprisingly, Mary remained boss of our barn lot until Daddy swapped her off in 1942.

Other than the times when she enforced her authority as top mule or bullied some timid soul trying to bridle her, Mary was calm and practically imperturbable. She never got flighty over loud noises, sudden movements, or strange odors. I don't believe she'd have taken more than passing notice of the devil himself, unless of course he showed up in the guise of a field hand. Certainly one of the truly amazing things about Old Mary was her reaction to snakes.

If anything can panic a horse or a mule, it's a predatory animal like a panther or a venomous snake. Panthers were gone from Ogeechee County by my time, but we still had more than our share of poisonous snakes, including the great diamondback rattler—a terrifying apparition six feet, or even more, in length.

The mowing and stacking of peavine hay in late summer, while a tough, sweaty chore for grownups, was a big event in the lives of rural kids. Hay was usually mowed starting at the edges of the field, forcing small animals lurking in the standing peavines to move inward ahead of the mower. When the last few swaths in the middle of the field were cut, the accumulated varmints had to skedaddle across barren ground for new cover. We could always count on catching a few young rabbits, a possum or two, and assorted sizes and colors of field mice. One year a full-grown bobcat broke from the hay and took off for the Horse Creek Swamp. Needless to say, none of us tried to stop that bundle of concentrated fury. Another time Ceroy Tolbert got sprayed by a polecat, a real funny thing for all except poor Ceroy.

One bright afternoon in September, 1936, Daddy mowed a twenty-acre hayfield behind our barn. Ceroy Tolbert and I had the task of tending the mowing teams. Mowing in warm weather is hard work for mules, so Daddy liked to switch teams in hourly relays. We delivered a rested team when Daddy called for one, and walked the retiring mules cool in the shade of a big oak tree. Mary and Lou made up one team, and they were spelled off by a pair of matched sorrel mules named Mutt and Jeff.

Late that afternoon Daddy mowed closer and closer to the short rounds. We hoped he'd be able to finish up before dark so that any game in the hay couldn't sneak off after sunset. At the far end of the field, Daddy turned to pick up a new swath. He'd hardly straightened out on the new round when he reined up and sat peering intently at the ground. We thought he might be about ready to signal for a new team, so we untied Mutt and Jeff and were about to trot them across the field when we saw Daddy jump down from the mower seat and flail away at something on the ground. We dropped the mules' reins and rushed over, and for the first time in my life I beheld a diamondback rattler.

That particular rattler was about four-and-a-half feet long, not overly big for its kind but still the most impressive snake I'd ever seen. As I stood staring at the writhing body, Daddy

23

pointed to another, smaller, one lying where it had been mangled by the mower blade. Daddy told us that the big rattler had rolled over the sickle bar and had lost its rattle in the process. He'd reined up immediately and had sat staring in horror as the snake slithered away between Mary's front hooves. He had fully expected to have a snakebit mule on his hands, but that diamondback was apparently of but one mind, and that was to escape.

If old Mary was at all disturbed by the proximity of that deadly serpent, she didn't show it. Perhaps strangest of all was Lou's reaction. Old Lou despised goats and had once dragged Deacon Tolbert's buggy off the road so that she could stomp an old nanny who'd gotten her head caught in a fence. Yet the heavy, goatlike musk of that rattler didn't perturb her in the least. Very likely mules can detect components of natural scents that the relatively feeble noses of humans miss.

We caught three rabbits that evening, along with a possum and three field mice—tiny, beige-colored sprites with white feet and tummies. However, those rattlers were by far the most spectacular varmints to come out of the hay that summer. I preserve a vivid image of the one Daddy laid low with his pitchfork—the chunky head with its grave smile, the stout body that seemed so reluctant to give up the ghost, and the elegant rhombs along the broad back. Many people bolt in terror at the sight of a diamondback. Others kill such venomous serpents on sight. Though they rank among the most dangerous of wild creatures, I've never had the heart to harm one. Their reluctance to use their deadly armament except in self-defense and their haughty, reserved manner command my respect, so I suffer them to go in peace.

One Saturday afternoon in the spring of 1936 we learned,

24

quite by accident, of Mary's origin. On market days Deacon Andrew Tolbert liked to drive Mary and Lou to town hitched to a two-horse wagon. That particular Saturday, just as he was about to tie the mules to a post in front of Cook's blacksmith shop, a stranger came up and asked if he could examine the black mule on the left. Deacon Tolbert explained that the mules were the property of Mr. J. B. Tolbert, his landlord, and pointed to Daddy, who happened to be talking with Deacon Josh Wiggins by the artesian well.

Daddy was surprised that a perfect stranger would be interested in one of his mules, and quite naturally asked the man for an explanation. The man, a Mr. Simpson, said that he thought he knew the mule, and if he was right, she would have a scar running across her forehead just above her eyes. Curious, Daddy examined Mary's forehead and found the scar precisely where Mr. Simpson had predicted it would be. That established, Mr. Simpson proceeded to tell his story.

He'd raised Mary, or Missy as he called her, from a colt. She had disappeared from his farm in the uplands of South Carolina in the fall of 1935. There had been a terrible drought that summer in the Piedmont, and Mr. Simpson's crops had failed. Not having any feed for his mules, he'd turned them out to forage as best they could along the roadsides. When Missy failed to come up one night, he assumed that she had finally perished to death. The scar had come from Missy's snagging her head on a barbed-wire fence.

Daddy then filled Mr. Simpson in on the remainder of Mary's story, explaining that he'd bought her from the Gypsies less than a week after Mr. Simpson had missed her. Evidently the Romanies had found her straggling along some country lane and had added her to their string without saying so much as

Pete Turkey to anyone. Had Old Missy had her strength, I'm sure those Gypsies would have been in for a surprise when they tried to bridle her.

Daddy offered to give Mary back or else pay Mr. Simpson a fair price for her. Mr. Simpson declined the offer with a laugh. He'd quit farming after the disaster of 1935, and had since made a good living drumming hardware and farm implements for a firm in Augusta. He said he had no use for a mule and wouldn't tell another mule to get up if it was sitting in his lap.

Mr. Simpson continued to sell hard goods in our community for several years and liked to take dinner with us when he was in town. He always went out to the barn lot to see Missy—as he continued to call her—when she came in from the fields at noon. Mary never showed any signs of wanting to get rambunctious with her former owner. Perhaps it was because she had forgotten him over the intervening years, or perhaps she sensed that he had no plans to put her to work. More likely it was because Mr. Simpson, like Deacon Andrew Tolbert, had her number, and she never forgot.

ROX, THE OUTLAW MULE

CONSIDERING the number of mules around in the old days, it is not surprising that a few could be dangerous if aroused. A very few were outlaws, animals dangerous under practically all circumstances. The only such mule that I ever knew well was Rox—a big, bay horse mule who was once the property of my Uncle Lester Tolbert.

Uncle Lester was just thirty years old in 1934 when he first started farming on his own. He liked to believe that he was as rugged as they came, and boasted around that he could outfight or outwrestle any man his size on the west side of Ogeechee County. Moreover, he could outplow any hand on his place and pick up to 400 pounds of cotton per day. With a family started and 350 acres of good land recently deeded over by his father, Old Cap'n Tolbert, there seemed to be no reason why my uncle shouldn't be content. Yet rumor had it that he was perpetually irked over the fact that his neighbors wouldn't credit him with any judgment when it came to picking mules.

Some suspected that my uncle's rancor stemmed from jealousy over Grandfather's talents as a judge of muleflesh. Be that as it may, when Uncle Lester came upon Rox, he was sure that at least some of the neighbors would have to sit up and take notice and concede that he was almost, if not quite, as good a picker of mules as the Old Cap'n himself.

Uncle Lester found Rox at Cribbens and Foxhall's stables in Dover, the county seat of Ogeechee County. A neighbor, Mr. Clay Parker, was along, and as Mr. Clay told it later, Uncle

Lester had been flabbergasted that the owners were willing to let such a big, strapping mule go for a paltry seventy-five dollars. Uncle Lester had forked over cash money for Rox before giving the jarhead so much as a precautionary look. Once the papers were signed, he led Rox out of his stall to read his teeth. Well, he never did ascertain the mule's age, for Rox came close to biting a few of my uncle's fingers off. Uncle Lester laid it down to nervousness, explaining to Mr. Clay that high-strung mules often turn fractious in strange surroundings. Once Old Rox had had a chance to settle down among other mules, he'd be all right. He would turn out to be a real man's mule, the kind you couldn't get ahold of any old day of the week. That much ascertained, they prodded Rox into Mr. Clay's truck and drove home.

The next morning Grandfather hitched up his buggy and drove over to check on his son's new mule. Old Cap'n Tolbert took one good look at Rox and shook his head. "Lester, this mule of yours worries me. He's got the makin's of an outlaw as sure as I'm born. He'll go on all right for a week or two, and then, when you ain't lookin' for it, all hell'll break loose. If that ever happens, and word gets around, you won't be able to get enough for him to set a jaybird up to a chaw of tobacco. He sounds to me like the same mule that tore up that loggin' camp up in Jenkins County a week or two back. Now if he was mine, I'd take him two or three counties over and see if I could get my money back."

Uncle Lester scoffed. "Oh come on now, Pa. You sure this is the same mule? I don't see nothin' about Old Rox that makes him look like no outlaw to me."

"Well, just look at the way he pokes his head at you with his ears back. Notice how he rolls his eyes so that you can see the whites around their rims? Anybody with any gumption knows that you can't trust a white-eyed mule."

"Let me tell you, Pa. I knew Rox was a tough customer when I bought him. Hell, that's the main reason I wanted him. I don't expect that this mule ever had a real man work him before. You just give me a week with him and I'll straighten the sonofabitch out, or know the reason why not."

Seeing no point in discussing the matter further, Grandfather climbed back into his buggy, wished his son luck, and drove home.

It was on a Sunday morning, three days after Uncle Lester had first turned Rox into the barn lot, before the big bay mule showed the first signs of the trouble to come. Deacon Tom Lawton, one of Uncle Lester's croppers, had an entitlement to use a mule to pull his buggy to church. That Sunday Deacon Lawton had sent his son Bubba up to the lot to catch out Old Rhodie, the deacon's favorite buggy mule. Young Bubba must have been fair terrorized when he looked up and saw a strange mule bearing down upon him practically spouting fire from both nostrils.

Uncle Lester was having breakfast at the time. When he heard the commotion in the barn lot, he dashed out onto the back porch just in time to see poor Bubba scramble over the lot fence with Rox chomping at his heels. Uncle Lester yelled, but Bubba lit a shuck for home without once looking back.

Grandfather and Uncle Lester were in agreement on at least one point: mules in need of discipline were best disciplined without delay. Perhaps a good forking was all Rox needed to change his notions about how a farm mule should act. By the time Uncle Lester had picked out his fork and stepped into the barn lot, Rox was steamed up and ready to fight anything that

29

walked, crept, or flew. Well, to make short of long, that hay-fork cooled him off in short order. After a little coaxing, Bubba came back and caught out his mule, but Rox's reputation as a bad actor was off and running.

Monday came, and Uncle Lester decided to see how his new mule took to siding cotton. Old Rox had had a bait of that fork for one week at least, so he settled down and let Uncle Lester hitch him to a single-stock grasshopper plow. Rox turned out to be some kind of plow mule. He stepped along about as lively as a young mare mule and turned the ends of the rows on the fly. Uncle Lester reined him tight and watched him closely, and between them they plowed a little more than five acres of seedling-sized cotton that first day, a fair-sized effort for anyone, man or mule.

Late that evening Uncle Lester turned a weary Rox into the barn lot, wolfed down his supper, and headed for town, itching for a chance to crow over his new mule. He found a knot of his cronies on the loafer's bench in front of Evans' General Store. He approached them grinning, hoping they'd ask him about his day with Rox. Daddy spoke first.

"Well, Lester, it looks like you're still in one piece. You must not of worked your new mule today."

Uncle Lester snorted. "Well by grabs, Jimmy, I did. We sided a little over five acres there where your and my fields butt up against each other. Best damned mule I ever saw."

Mr. Clay Parker spoke. "You know, Lester, that mule acted mighty funny over there at Cribbens and Foxhall's stables. Your pa claims he's got the makin's of an outlaw. I ain't never known him to be wrong about anything like that."

"Yeah, Clay, I know. Pa wants me to get rid of him. But let me tell you. Old Rox is a little rough. I had to fork him once, but I'll guaran-damn-tee you he'll be tame by the end of this week, if the rain holds off. The main trouble with that mule is he ain't never had no real man to work him before."

Deacon Josh Wiggins came by and stopped. The men grew silent, waiting for the good deacon to offer his opinion of the new mule.

"Lester, they tell me you went out and bought a dinged outlaw."

Uncle Lester smirked at the way gossip spreads. "Now, Mr. Josh, who went and told you a thing like that?"

"Your pa did. Dinged if I can understand why you boys don't pay more attention to your pa. Look, I've seen outlaw mules maim people. That dinged rascal'll get you when you ain't expectin' it. You better do like your pa says and get shet of him before somebody around your place gets hurt."

"Mr. Josh, I respect Pa's word and yours, too. You know that. But Old Rox is a real man's mule, the kind you can't get ahold of any old day of the week. I'll make a Christian out of him just like I told Pa I would. You just watch me."

Deacon Josh shook his head. "Well, I hope you can, Lester. I sure wouldn't want to hear that he hurt you bad. Good night, gentlemen."

Rox behaved well enough for the remainder of that week until Friday at noon. Then, as Daddy described it, all hell broke loose in Uncle Lester's cotton field. Daddy had been checking over some cotton he'd had bunched out by some wage hands from town when he heard a streak of cussing that could have come only from his baby brother. Daddy looked up just in time to see Rox bolt from a huge dust cloud and take off hell bent for a scope of woods at the end of Uncle Lester's cotton field. The dust settled some and Uncle Lester staggered out,

31

yelling and shaking his fist at the fleeing mule. Daddy rushed over, calmed his brother, and asked just what in tarnation had happened.

As near as my uncle could figure, he'd committed the error of taking his eyes off Rox just as they'd made the turn for home at noon. Old Rox, ever alert for a chance to run away, had most likely been peeping back on the sly. The second Uncle Lester let his guard down, that mule had bagged out like a scalded cat in search of a chinaberry tree.

Uncle Lester had the habit of wrapping the right plow line around his wrist when he sided cotton. As a result, he got tangled up in the plow lines when Rox bolted, and was dragged for more than a hundred yards before he was able to shake loose. Daddy said later it was a blue-eyed wonder that his brother hadn't been dragged raw or else chopped to giblets by the flying plow sweep. But all he suffered from the mishap was a rope-burned wrist and a severely ruffled dignity. Later, when he and some of his hands finally cornered Rox, the outlaw had shucked all of his gear except the collar. They had to choke him down with plow lines and lead him home with a nose twitch. Even after that he still wanted to fight.

The aftermath of the runaway episode proved most embarrassing for Uncle Lester. Half of his plow hands were ready to quit, and practically all of the neighbors were laughing behind his back. Obviously he had to get rid of Rox and then lie low for a spell if he was to preserve even the semblance of face in the community. Maybe Rox was better cut out for logging than for farm work. He had the size, and the Old Cap'n had hinted that Rox had had experience in a logging camp. That reasoned out, Uncle Lester tied Rox to the back of a two-horse wagon and drove down to the Burke Lumber

Company to see if Mr. Prince Burke, the owner, would take Rox off his hands.

Mr. Burke called his teamsters and log snakers out to look Rox over. None of them said as much, but their evasive looks told Mr. Burke that word of Rox's ways had preceded the outlaw to the mill site. Mr. Burke agreed that Rox had the makings of a logging mule, but explained that he couldn't ask his crews to work a mule they were afraid of. Uncle Lester was about ready to leave for home when Silas West, a timber cart driver, stepped forward and asked permission to make a deal for Rox. Mr. Burke pondered for a moment, nodded, and Silas swapped a black mule named Zelda for Rox. Thus did Rox the outlaw begin his short-lived career as a logging mule.

Silas West was a most remarkable man. More than seven feet tall, he towered over most, yet he was about the gentlest man I ever knew. I never saw him when there wasn't a grin on his alert black face. He knew just about all there was to know about hunting and fishing, and was always ready with a story for us kids. He could also conjure away warts but was best known for his skills as a teamster, and he drew top wages for his work.

Before crawler tractors came into general use in the woods, timber carts hauled logs to peckerwood sawmills, or to staging areas where the timbers were loaded onto trucks or log wagons. A timber cart was a simple contrivance, consisting mostly of two iron-tired wheels on short axles fitted into a U-shaped frame. A short tongue jutted out from the top of the frame. When the cart was in motion this tongue angled downward so that its end dragged the ground. The end of the tongue rode on a stout dragpin called a foot. The foot was made of some kind of hardwood, such as persimmon or dogwood, and was jammed through the clevis at the end of the tongue, slanting backwards. This meant that a timber cart could only be drawn forward and not backed up unless the tongue was lifted. A pair of stout dog irons, called *hounds* in the logging trade, dangled beneath the inverted U-frame. These were for gripping assorted sizes of timber.

When loading a bolt of saw timber, the cart's tongue was raised so that the hounds dropped down over the bolt. Once the hounds were set to bite into the log, the tongue was pulled down to rest once more on the ground. As the tongue was lowered, the hounds gripped the log, lifting it from the ground. The log was then further secured for transporting by toggling a log chain around it.

When a timber cart was pitched upward to grip a timber, there was a danger that the U-frame might flop over backwards on the hand setting the hounds. To prevent that, a tipped cart was propped on a stout scantling called a lazy boy. Once a log was dogged and chained, the driver hitched a heavy rope to the tongue so that the team could trip the cart. That done, the driver set the double tree to the clevis and pulled stakes for the mill. I've seen whole pine trees, 100 feet in length, being hauled by a tandem hitch of four stout mules.

Depending upon the terrain and the size of the timber, two, three, four, or even six mules might be worked to a cart. Silas West used four mules, hitched to his cart as two teams in tandem. The left-hand, or on, leader is the boss mule in a tandem hitch. Silas's leader was a plump, iron-gray mule named Ada. Silas rode directly behind her on the left-hand wheeler, and controlled her and the off-leader with reins, although I've heard it claimed that he actually directed Old Ada with voice signals. With an intelligent, responsive mule like Ada at the head of his span, Silas could maneuver his cart through tight places in the woods with a minimum expenditure of time and energy, and thus haul a bit more timber in a day's time than the average driver.

Silas started Rox up front at off-leader with the intention of moving him to off-wheeler once he'd learned the ways of the woods. Silas called Ada his teacher, and he always put a new mule up front beside her for breaking in. In educating Rox, both Silas and Ada had their work cut out. The outlaw worked well when he felt like it, but never stopped acting up in harness if that suited his notion. At times he'd lay back in his traces, or else bite and kick at his teammates. Silas took to carrying a stout hickory pole to prod Rox when he threatened to get out of hand. However, the old teamster had to be careful how he used the prod, for if he touched Rox up too much, that jarhead would take off and try to pull the cart by himself.

With time, Silas came to be pleased with Rox's performance, if not overjoyed. Some Monday mornings Silas had to enlist the help of two or three mill hands to hitch Rox up, but all things considered, the old mule-skinner came to feel that in swapping for Rox he'd struck a good bargain.

Unlike Uncle Lester, Silas West never let his guard down around Rox. I heard him tell Daddy once that getting careless around Rox was like laying your life on the line. Rox was especially touchy about having his hooves tampered with. Logging mules ordinarily wore heavy shoes to protect their hooves in the rough going through roots and stumps. Rox was never shod, nor could anyone recall a time when a farrier dressed his hooves. Swint Fuller looked after the Burke Company teams on a more or less routine basis, but Rox was one mule the old horse doctor wouldn't touch.

In the old days logs were loaded onto conveyances by rolling them up a pair of stout poles, called skids, on a system of chains.

The ends of a medium log chain were toggled through sturdy eyebolts driven into the truck bed on either side of the skids. The center of the chain was laid out on the ground between the poles so that its middle formed a belly. A log was then rolled over the belly so that the middle of the chain could be lapped over the log. On the other side of the truck, a team hitched to a length of chain called a stretcher waited. Once a log had been lapped, the loader tossed the stretcher chain over the truck bed so that a hook on its end could be attached to the belly of the lap. Once the hook was set, the loader clucked to his team and the log rolled up the skids as pretty as you please.

Loading a big timber was a pretty fair task for the average team. Rox could load logs by his lonesome, in single harness. Sometimes when he took to cutting up at the cart, Silas put him to loading logs to cool him off. One afternoon Uncle Lester watched Rox load sixteen-foot logs as fast as trucks could haul them away. According to my uncle, Rox was so fast on the takeoff, once the stretcher hook was set, that he came close on one occasion to pinning the hook man to the truck bed.

I only saw Rox working timber a few times. I remember a sultry morning in July when Daddy and I stopped at the Phillips place to watch the Burke crews fell big longleaf pines. As we watched a crosscut saw bite into one of those tall, slick-barked trees, Silas's cart inched up a knoll below us with a thick, sixteen-foot cut in its hounds. Up front Rox and Ada tugged and groaned with their tongues lolling over their bits. It looked to me as if the two were pulling most of the load by themselves.

Once up the rise, Silas grunted and the traces went slack. All the mules except Rox seemed grateful for a chance to blow. He fidgeted and stomped around, showing every sign that he was fed up with all the heat, flies, and hard labor. Silas growled and fingered the prod. That seemed to settle the outlaw down so that afterwards he took his rest more calmly.

Once the mules had had a good blow out, Silas clucked, and the cart started to move. Hardly had the traces tightened before Rox planted his hooves, throwing the span into stamping confusion. Silas leaned forward and caught the outlaw a smart lick across the croup. That got Rox moving; he took off in a near trot, practically pulling the cart by himself.

The staging bed was only about a hundred yards away, but before the cart had traveled half the distance, it was one hundred percent obvious that Rox had no intention of stopping. Silas leaped from the on-wheeler's back yelling, "Hold him, Ada!" Ada and the wheelers sat back in their traces and tried to check Rox, but that powerful mule kept struggling and managed to tug the cart, mules and all, for another ten yards before Silas got him under control.

Silas came out of the fracas with a bloodied face, the work of one of Rox's hooves. Daddy wanted Silas to see a doctor, but the old teamster would have none of it. He wiped the blood away with a sweaty bandana and doused the wound with coal oil. Daddy studied Rox, by then standing quietly while the loading crew rolled the log away with big cant hooks.

"Silas, you know that damned mule came close to killin' my brother once. Ain't it a little risky the way you fool around with him?"

Silas chuckled. "Naw, Cap'n. There ain't no harm in Old Rox if you know how to handle him. He just gets a little lively now and then. It takes a real man to work that mule."

Daddy nodded, and we drove home to dinner.

Rox met his end that fall, a death that was as tragic as it was untimely. The Burke company leased a block of timber on the Gunn property that summer, and Silas had the task of carting logs up the ridge that flanks the north bank of Big Horse Creek. By then Rox had graduated to off-wheeler, and a new mule had taken his place up front by Ada.

One morning in late September, as the span struggled up the ridge with a big poplar log, the left wheel of the cart got jammed behind a large gum sapling. Because a timber cart can't be backed to clear an obstruction, Silas dismounted and took an ax to the sapling while the span held firm in their traces. Silas hadn't chopped more than half a dozen licks before Rox's right hind hoof slid into a hole that contained a huge yellow jacket nest. Before Silas realized what was happening, the span was pitching and bucking in screaming pandemonium.

Silas rushed from mule to mule, shucking breast chains and slashing hame strings. He managed to cut all of the mules loose except Rox. The stings of those fierce wasps roused all of the outlaw's instincts for violence, and Silas couldn't get near enough to him to set him free. As it was, Old Silas stayed with his mule as long as he dared, and paid for his loyalty by spending a week in bed with his eyes swollen shut.

Two days passed before the Burke crews mustered the courage to go in after the timber cart. They found Rox still hitched to the off-wheel. Before that powerful jarhead died, he had managed to tug the cart free, only to have it get tangled up again in a wind-thrown oak less than a hundred yards from where Silas had been forced to abandon him. On hearing the news of Rox's last struggle, Silas asked that the outlaw be buried where he had fallen; and he was, on the hillside near a big tulip poplar.

Just recently Daddy and I took time off to go fishing in Big Horse Creek. We didn't catch much that day. The old creek is just not the fishing hole it once was. Besides that, it was too fine a day to concentrate on anything as listless as a fishing pole. The tulip poplars were in bloom, and I spent most of the time lying on my back gazing up at the bees as they buzzed among the green and gold flowers, sipping the spicy nectar. Bees are, of course, cousins to yellow jackets and, like them, can be fierce if aroused. That particular day they seemed intent only upon gathering the sweets of the wild.

On the way home Daddy showed me Rox's grave. The tulip tree is gone, a victim of lightning I was told. In its place are three young pines, stately saplings, perhaps reminiscent of the mule that sleeps beneath their roots.

Rox was not my kind of mule. I never cottoned to the dangerous, unpredictable kind. Perhaps Uncle Lester and Silas West had something to prove when they chose to work a tough customer like Old Rox, but I never felt the need for such a trying challenge. Still, I admire Old Rox for many of the things he was, stately and proud, fabulously strong and intelligent, a jarhead with a special kind of character, one that never bent to the will of man the taskmaster without putting up a determined scrap.

BELLE, A MULE WHO KNEW
HER WAY HOME

MANKIND has ever marveled at the homing instincts of those he regards as lesser creatures. What mysterious force allows a pigeon to find its way back unerringly to the loft? To cite some more spectacular cases, how do tiny birds, some no bigger than a person's thumb, navigate from the Canadian Arctic to the tropics and back, year after year? Just about everybody is aware of the homing abilities of birds, but I dare say there are many who don't know that some four-footed animals are pretty good direction-finders in their own right.

Mules spent their entire lives in confinement, or else in harness, so one might have expected that those animals would be totally bewildered if they found themselves in strange places with no familiar faces around. But that was not necessarily the case. Many mules had a well-developed sense of home-finding, though I'm not prepared to claim that the cleverest mule in that regard was the equal of even the most bumbling pigeon. Still, a few were pretty good. In his book *If Nothin' Don't Happen*, R. M. Newell tells of an old gray mule who must have been mighty hard to lose. A couple of lads rode the old plug out one night intent upon jacklighting a deer. Well, the old gray circled back home on them, and before the hunters realized where they were, they'd decimated their grandmother's herd of pet goats.

In the fall of 1912 a drygoods drummer from Augusta

showed up at Grandfather's place with one of his team lame. The Old Cap'n loaned him a mule named Claymore, and agreed to keep the drummer's mule until its leg mended. A week later Claymore showed up at the barn-lot gate with nothing on but a halter. It developed that Old Claymore had slipped his tether rope three days before and had struck a bee-line for home, some sixty miles away. As far as I'm aware, that trek of Claymore's stands as a record for mules.

My own experience with home-finding in mules covers just a few cases, the most spectacular of which doubtless concerned a mule of Daddy's named Belle. Belle was what we called a cotton mule—the trim, long-legged kind bred in the hills of eastern Tennessee. I remember her as being brownish-black in color with the white ring around her muzzle seen so commonly in dark-colored mules. Daddy admired the way she stepped out to a single-stock plow, but my main interest in her was as a riding mule. Old Belle sat better than a lot of saddle horses I've ridden, and she was so steady I could fire a shotgun from her back. In fact, it was while out hunting with Belle that I learned of her remarkable homing ability.

Open range was legal in Ogeechee County back in the casual days of the 1930s. That meant that cows, hogs, and goats were free to roam at will while farmers struggled to keep them fenced out of cultivated land. The byways and woodlands were positively crawling with armies of cows and pigs. Even the town streets were choked with the hungry brutes. Many a Saturday I've been with Daddy when he had to drive around hogs wallowing in mudholes on Main Street, or listened to him fume over having to honk cows over in the town square. Hordes of lean shoats roamed the grounds of the Millerville Grammar School during the lunch hour, cleaning up scraps. Those pigs were as alert to the dinner bell as we pupils were, and able to negotiate the cattle guards at the entrances better than most of us.

In those depression-ridden days it was hard enough for the average farmer to meet his notes, much less find the cash to buy new fence wire when the old rusted away. For many it was a matter of patch and make do and chase the neighbors' pigs the whole summer long. Daddy was forced to chuckle every time he saw Deacon Josh Wiggins ride by. Deacon Josh was one of the few who could afford to fence his own pigs out. Consequently, the good deacon spent a lot of time checking up on how his hogs were faring in other people's cornfields.

My parents owned about fifty head of cows back then. About a dozen were well-bred Jersey and Guernsey milch stock, whereas the remainder were what local folks called Poland Chinas. Now many have heard of the Poland China breed of swine. I doubt that nearly as many have heard of Poland China cattle. Well, Poland Chinas were those scrubby, half-wild beasts seen so commonly in the South during the days of open range. Poland Chinas tended, among other undesirable traits, to be long on horn and short on beef, and as tough as the rawhide that bound their bones.

Well-bred milkers produced far more than their scrubby sisters, so the local farmers were naturally inclined to take the best care of their best stock. During cold weather Jerseys and Guernseys were fed peavine hay and cottonseed meal, whereas Poland Chinas had to pretty much rustle for themselves. As winter wore on, natural forages got scarce and scrub stock got thin, some few practically getting down on the lift. Then, as some wags put it, the forlorn beasts had to be propped up with poles for milking, and one of them could be milked dry into a china teacup.

Our Poland Chinas, being more or less wild to begin with, were forever straying off to the thickets and canebrakes of the Ogeechee River bottoms. There were times when they didn't come up for weeks on end. Some folks around home felt that just about any livestock was fair game, so we liked to keep an eye on our cows, whether well bred or not. That suited me just fine, because it gave me the perfect excuse to saddle up Belle and take off to round up those Poland Chinas. I especially liked to punch those lean critters during the hunting season, for I bagged many a plump squirrel while going through the motions of driving those cows home.

One Friday afternoon in late September of 1937, I proffered the lame excuse of riding off to round up cattle in order to get in some hunting in the Ogeechee bottoms. I found no Poland Chinas that day—not that I looked overly hard for any—but did manage to bag two plump cat squirrels. In fact, I became so absorbed in stalking those bushytails that I lost track of my whereabouts. Almost before I realized what was happening, I was fair lost, hardly aware of the difference between up and down.

As those who've been lost in a dense forest know, it's an eerie feeling, one bordering on panic. Shadows were stretching out, and neither boy nor mule had the foggiest notion of where home lay, or so I believed at the time. As it developed, Belle knew better.

Probably because Belle was with me, I didn't panic. I kept my head, woozy and swimmy though it was, and tried mightily to sort out my sense of direction, but the more we wandered about the more I realized that we were merely traveling in circles. I even tried the old Boy Scout trick of examining the moss on the sides of trees, but as it turned out, those swamp trees had about as much moss on one side as on the other. Not knowing what better to do, I reined Belle up on a spruce pine hammock and tried spying out familar landmarks, but the more I peered, the more objects and directions merged into one puzzling mosaic of sight and impression. Then Belle started tossing her head up and down and pawing the ground, a sure sign that a mule is bored and wants to do something other than stand around and fret. A few moments later she moved off without my permission, a thing she'd never done before.

My first impulse was to rebuke her, but I held up. Mosquitoes were out, and anyone who's ever ridden a mule into a swamp during warm weather knows that those lowland gallernippers prefer the gore of the mount to that of the rider any evening of the week. I had to agree with Belle that it was better to keep moving than to stay in one place and be eaten alive. Besides, by then I was aware that I could do no better than my mule about finding our way home, so I gave Belle her head.

I lost count of the time we spent winding around in that swamp, slogging through stagnant creeks and stumbling through cat-brier thickets. Darkness had long since fallen, and I could have sworn that those gallernippers had telegraphed all of their relatives. Except for the chirping of a few random crickets and the perpetual buzz of all those mosquitoes, that swamp was quiet. There were no roosters crowing or dogs barking or any other familiar sounds that would have cheered me. Once an owl hooted overhead, scaring the daylights out of me. Belle didn't even flinch. She just plodded along as if she knew precisely what she was about. At the time, I wished that I could have been as sure.

Suddenly Belle quickened her pace and stepped out onto a road that looked somewhat familiar in the light of the newly risen moon. However, I was still too bewildered to be sure.

44

Another half-mile or so and we passed a house, and two dogs rushed out to bark at us. One of them sounded like Deacon Andrew Tolbert's Black Gal, and that heartened me no end. Up ahead a mule brayed. Belle broke into a trot and brayed back. Then I knew we were home.

I unsaddled Belle, gave her water, and stabled her with plenty of hay and oats. I gulped down a dipper of water and dragged off to bed, too bone-weary and sore to worry about food.

Daddy woke me late the next morning. He said that he and Mama had been worried when I hadn't shown up for supper, but since they'd always relied upon my using my judgment to stay out of trouble, they'd not waited up for me. I told Daddy of our adventure, and he was so impressed that he decided to put Belle's home-finding ability to a test.

The next Sunday afternoon Daddy rode Belle into the Ogeechee bottoms with me following along on Old Alec. We crisscrossed our trail and took particular note of trees and other landmarks along the way. When Daddy finally gave Belle free rein, she backtracked along her own trail, not missing a turn.

I was with Daddy the following Saturday when he told the gang that hung around Cook's blacksmith shop about Belle's amazing feat. Although few seemed impressed, several were ready to offer comment. Mr. Dawse Cook allowed that he was familiar with backtracking in mules, declaring that they were able to do it by sniffing out their own tracks. Sam Catoe disagreed, claiming instead that a mule found its way back along a trail by memorizing landmarks along the way. For evidence he cited the fact that Fent Newsome's Old Pender Jane could follow any weed-grown trail in the Ogeechee bottoms and never stray off on the wrong fork, even if Fent happened to be dozing on the wagon seat. The old gray plug couldn't depend on her nose to guide her because the moonshine Fent hauled on his wagon outstunk everything else around, including Fent himself.

When Tooky Calhoun pointed out that mules like Belle and Pender Jane could follow a trail about as well by night as by day, Sam headed him off by explaining that mules switched over to their night eyes after dark.

A mule's night eyes are those little hornlike patches (called chestnuts by horsemen) on the inner sides of the front legs just above the knees. Horses have chestnuts on both the front and hind legs, whereas mules, like asses, have them on the fore-legs only. The precise function of the scruffy little patches is not known, if indeed there is any. Some hot air merchants put up a job that horses and mules use them to see with at night.

I asked Sam Catoe if it was easier to slip up on a mule than a horse after dark, inasmuch as a mule is bound to be blind in the hind legs. Old Sam declined to answer, stating merely that anybody who'd try to sneak up on the hind end of either a horse or a mule at night was just a plain damned fool. Be that as it may, the night-eye theory broke up the argument, mainly because no one could top it, and so to this very day I don't know how mules find their way home in daylight, much less in the dark.

MR. CLYDE AND OLD BILL

OLD BELLE was some kind of clever mule when it came to backtracking and finding her way home. A few other mules I've known were pretty good at home-finding, though I never saw another that compared with Belle. Bill—a big, bay horse mule who belonged to our neighbor, Mr. Clyde Tilly—developed homing instincts out of necessity, inasmuch as there were times when his owner was unable to drive him. Eventually those treks under slack reins led to tragic consequences for Mr. Clyde, but I never blamed Old Bill. After all, one can hardly expect a mule to be its master's keeper.

I first met Mr. Clyde and Old Bill one blustery afternoon in February, 1935. At the time Daddy and Grandfather were talking at the artesian well in the town square while I fidgeted around trying to work up the courage to ask Daddy for another nickel. A green Jersey wagon drove up. The driver, a tall man past middle age, got down, patted his mule on the nose, and came over. After a round of handshaking, the man introduced himself as Mr. Clyde Tilley and said that he had driven over from South Carolina looking for a place to settle. He would be mighty obliged if the gentlemen could put him onto a one-horse farm with a dwelling house that he could rent cheap.

Daddy and Grandfather tipped their hats to Mrs. Tilley, a smallish woman in a poke bonnet, and advised Mr. Tilley to see the Widow Barbour, who lived on Back Street. Daddy

47

even offered to help Mr. Tilley negotiate with the widow, but the old gentleman thanked us and said that he couldn't see putting such accommodating folks to any more trouble. That done, he pressed a nickel into my hand and drove off. Gifts from strangers were taboo in my family, but by then Mr. Clyde didn't seem like a stranger anymore.

Few in the market-day crowd paid more than passing notice to the Tilleys. The country was filled with penniless drifters fleeing the Depression, and to most, the Tilleys must have looked like more of the same. However, the old couple settled in on their rented acreage, and before long the local folks accepted Mr. Clyde as a friendly, though somewhat shiftless, sort of man. Miss Nettie, as Mrs. Tilley came to be called, rarely ventured out into public. In a land where people were inclined to accept embellished rumor over humdrum fact, Miss Nettie's reluctance to socialize touched off the suspicion that she was off in the head.

We kids grew to love Mr. Clyde. When it came to spinning yarns and fishing, he had no peer, and he never seemed too busy to join my pals and me along Big Horse Creek to try for big redbreast or channel cats. Some suspected that Mr. Clyde's love of fishing accounted for the size of the weeds in his fields. Deacon Josh Wiggins was certain, and being the kind of man who could tolerate neither sin nor sloth, allowed that he'd be dinged if Mr. Clyde wouldn't rather shoot the breeze and fish than tend his crops. For once in my recollection, just about everybody had to agree that the good deacon had a point.

As was the case with most rural folks of his time, Saturday was the big day of Mr. Clyde's week. And like most, he showed up in town decked out in his Sunday-go-to-meeting best. Mr. Clyde's market-day itinerary became about as predictable as the phases of the moon. He usually arrived in town around three o'clock, tied Old Bill to a hitching post in front of Cook's blacksmith shop, and headed around to Evans' General Store. After charging the few groceries Miss Nettie needed, he'd set each of us kids up to a sack of grab-bag candy. For that we gratefully toted his groceries around to his wagon. Then, with all pressing business out of the way, Mr. Clyde would plop down by the potbellied stove in the middle of the store and swap yarns with his cronies until closing time. Or, if the weather was warm, he'd drift back over to the blacksmith shop and spend the afternoon with the loafers who gathered there on Saturdays.

Mock abuse characterized rustic humor in Mr. Clyde's day. The uninitiated might believe that the participants in those quarrels were bitter enemies when, in fact, they were often the best of friends. Mr. Clyde could dish out bogus insults with the best of them; that is, until he began to wear down around early dusk. Then he was likely to take exception to some of the jibes, and that led to even more pressure from the likes of Sam Catoe and Foots Mathis. When that happened, Mr. Clyde would stalk out in a huff and go over to Fails' Cafe to drown his tensions in Fent Newsome's white lightning. An hour or so later he'd show up at Evans' General Store, mumbling drunk.

Mr. Fate Evans was a kindly man, but he drew the line at letting drunks stagger in and out of his store. Even when soused, Mr. Clyde was polite enough to acknowledge Mr. Fate's right to keep his place of business orderly, so the old gentleman would settle on the loafer's bench outside and proceed to pass out. At closing time, Mr. Fate would send some of us kids around to the blacksmith shop to get Mr. Clyde's wagon. Then he and some of the standers-by would lay the old fellow into his wagon and give Bill his head. That mule would head straight home and stand braying by the front gate. Although I know

Miss Nettie dreaded those episodes, she would dutifully get up, take Bill out of harness, and help her husband to bed.

Those homeward jaunts of Bill's under slack reins became a kind of tradition around our community, the kind of happening people came to expect on a more or less routine basis. One of the few times the routine was disrupted followed a Saturday night when my cousin, Clint Parker, and some of his roughneck cronies got biggety and shot out some street lights.

When Mayor Jim Skinner heard about the shoot-out, he was as mad as a tromped-on rattler. He called the town council together and demanded an appropriation to hire a town constable as a necessary and proper step in breaking up some of the damned foolishness that was threatening to take over. Most of the council members demurred, feeling that the usual run of Saturday night devilment led to no enduring harm. If something really bad happened, there was always Sheriff Barnwell Tate to be called. However, as those who knew Mr. Jim will recall, the mayor could be mighty persuasive when he set his mind to it. After haranguing the council for a solid hour on public malfeasance and on dereliction of duty in general, the mayor got his appropriation.

No one around Millerville wanted the job of town constable, so Mayor Skinner had to go over into Buford County to find a willing candidate. The new constable, a Mr. Mutt Lange, reported for duty the following Saturday. He was a tall, cadaverous-looking fellow, kind of like some of the frontier marshals we'd seen in cowboy movies. As if to heighten further his image as a tough lawman, Mr. Lange wore a wide-brimmed stetson hat and a loud western vest. His armament consisted of a homemade billy club, evidently the end of a rake handle loaded with lead, and an old Owlhead revolver jammed into a holster that looked as if it had recently housed some child's cap pistol.

Constable Lange patrolled the streets with all the dignity he could muster, and he needed plenty with people guffawing and flapping their pants and yelling "Ride 'em, cowboy" and "Howdy, podner." I never recalled seeing so many people drunk, or at least staggering through the motions of being loaded. Fent Newsome shook a pint of raw moon under the constable's nose and then laughed when Mr. Lange threatened to run him in. Worst of all was when Clint Parker and his pals rushed around to Main Street yelling that the bank had been robbed. Constable Lange already had his pistol out of the holster before he recalled that we didn't even have a bank in Millerville.

I had just walked out of Evans' General Store when I saw the constable and Mayor Skinner lift Mr. Clyde from the loafer's bench and tote him off in the direction of the town calaboose. Later I learned that the old fellow had been arrested on a charge of public drunkenness and disorderly conduct. I could sympathize with Mr. Lange. He needed to prove to himself that he was actually a stern lawman, but what I couldn't understand was how he and the mayor had decided that Mr. Clyde was disorderly, when they had to help him to jail.

The next morning Daddy and I drove down to the calaboose to bail Mr. Clyde out. We found him sober, though bleary-eyed and shaky from the night before. He apologized to Daddy for our finding him in jail, and swore that he was off strong drink for life. Constable Lange took Daddy's ten dollars bail money and reminded my father that he was responsible for Mr. Clyde's appearance in court the following Saturday night at eight o'clock sharp. Mr. Clyde, in his turn, assured us that there need be no worry over him; he'd stay sober and show up in court without any prompting on our part.

Saturday night rolled around, and Mayor Skinner, serving in his alternate role as Judge of Recorder's Court, convened judicial proceedings in the white waiting room at the depot. The first case involved two black citizens who were up for cussing in public and drawing knives on each other. Judge Skinner accepted Constable Lange's testimony over their pleas of innocence, and fined them two dollars each. The judge then commanded Mr. Clyde Tilley to appear before the bench to answer to a charge of drunk and disorderly conduct. However, it was soon evident that Mr. Clyde was not going to appear, at least not voluntarily.

When Constable Lange found the defendant, he was at his accustomed place on the loafer's bench, far too drunk to stand trial. On getting that news, Judge Skinner entered a plea of prayer for judgment continued, and declared Daddy's bail money forfeited. Later Mr. Fate Evans told Daddy that he'd overheard Judge Skinner tell Constable Lange to lay off the old sot since he was harmless and, in any case, too poor to pay fines.

That December the Widow Barbour sold her land to the Comer Timber and Land Company and retired to Florida. That big outfit had no time for penny-ante leaseholders like the Tilleys, so Mr. Clyde had to look for a new situation. Because the old fellow was likely to be careless about paying his rent on time, no one with any land to spare wanted to deal with him. After a lot of persuasion, Daddy was able to get Deacon Josh Wiggins to agree to lease the Tilleys sixty acres on a year-to-year basis, but only after Daddy had agreed to put up half a year's rent in advance and cosign a note for the rest.

My brothers and I helped the Tilleys move to their new

place. Driving Old Bill hitched to that green wagon was fun. Only two trips were needed to move all their household goods over. After we'd finished, Mr. Clyde offered each of us a quarter. We thanked him and said that we would feel more than repaid if, come spring, he took us out fishing on the Ogeechee River in his boat.

Mr. Clyde didn't show up in town the following Saturday, but arrived at his usual time the next, complaining of having been down with a touch of grippe. He got soused, as was his custom, and at closing time Mr. Fate Evans, as was his custom, helped the aged inebriate into his wagon and pointed Bill toward the road for home.

Near daybreak the next morning our household was awakened by a pounding at our front door. Daddy and I got up to see who was paying us such an early, or late, call, depending upon how one chose to look at it. We found Miss Nettie Tilley at the door. She was plenty alarmed but remained outwardly calm as she told us that Mr. Clyde had not returned from town the night before.

We couldn't recall hearing that the old fellow had been arrested again, so it looked to us as if something bad might have happened. Daddy thought for a moment and asked, "Miss Nettie, was yesterday the first time that Mr. Tilley drove Bill to town from your new place?"

"Yes, Mr. Tolbert. Yesterday was the first time that Mr. Tilley ever went to town from our new home."

Realization of what had most likely happened dawned upon the three of us in a flash. We wasted no time pondering the matter further. Instead, we piled into our old Ford and lit out for the Barbour place. We arrived to find Bill standing by the front-yard gate, waiting, as was his custom, for somebody to take him out.

That mule brayed with joy when we drove up, but there wasn't anything to be joyful about. That particular morning was the coldest of the year, well below freezing, and Mr. Clyde was in a bad way from exposure. We bundled him up in some croaker sacks we found in the wagon, and rushed him to the county hospital. The doctors there did what they could for him, but the night in the open wagon had brought on double pneumonia, and that, along with the ravages of poverty, age, and rotgut likker, proved to be too much for the old man. Mr. Clyde Tilley died two days later.

Mr. Clyde was buried on Christmas Eve. For the grave site Reverend Martin chose a little knoll in the Baptist cemetery overlooking a place on Big Horse Creek where Mr. Clyde had liked to take us kids fishing. There weren't many people at the funeral, and Miss Nettie was the only woman I saw in the small gathering. I served as a pallbearer. I didn't know it at the time, but it was one of the community's ways of recognizing that I was on the threshold of manhood.

Three days after the funeral Miss Nettie paid us another call. She wanted to sell Bill and the wagon and use the money to go back to South Carolina to live near her son, a doctor in Columbia. She explained that her son had sent her money along to keep her and Mr. Clyde going. Daddy offered her seventy-five dollars for the mule and wagon, a sum she gladly accepted, and thus did the Tilleys pass from our lives. Old Bill lived on with us for several more years, a patient and steady mule, well worth his hay and oats. While with us he never again had to venture out into the public road to find his way home under slack reins, but I bet he could have, had the need ever arisen.

PENDER JANE

GRANDFATHER and his friends admired stylish mules, the kind that stood tall, looked proud, and pranced along with their ears pricked forward, but not all jarheads were gifted with style. Some, like my daddy's old humpbacked plug, Alec, never had any to begin with, whereas age, the great equalizer, robbed others of any stylish bearings they might have had in their youth. I've always believed that Old Pender Jane fitted into the latter category.

When I knew Pender Jane she was already old, anywhere between twenty and forty unless I miss my guess. Her coat was rough and unkempt, with the gall marks of decades of trace chains etched in bold relief on her flanks. She was slow of foot, as befits the aged, and her long ears flopped back and forth when she walked. Folks described her as a gray, although I remember her as being dead-white in color, at least after a heavy rain. Still, her coal-black nose suggested that she might have been iron-gray in her earlier years. Ordinary though she may have looked, Old Pender Jane nonetheless remains one of the most remarkable mules I have ever known.

Some claim that the personalities and even the looks of people and their pets merge over time. That might be the case with some people and their dogs, but it's definitely not so with mules and the people who work them. Jarheads are content to go their own way and remain as individualistic as their masters, or maybe even more so. That's the way it was with Pender Jane and her owner, Fent Newsome, the kingpin bootlegger around Millerville when I was a lad. True, both were rough and seedy in appearance, but beyond that any resemblance between the two faltered. Fent was short and dumpy behind his faded overalls and black wool hat, whereas his mule was rangy and ribby-poor. Moreover, Old Jane was meek and mild in disposition, while her master was inclined to be sullen and mean.

We kids regarded Fent Newsome as double-distilled evil, especially when he pinned us with his red, squinty eyes. Yet I wouldn't be telling the whole truth if I claimed that the man's stare was wholly malevolent, there being a hint of desperation in it, kind of like that of a lean shoat I'd seen once who was having an increasingly tough time minding other pigs away from his trough.

It's easy to understand why a pig beset by an army of hungry rivals trying to steal his swill would be desperate. Fent Newsome's trepidation was a little harder to figure. The man had no competition worth mentioning, and he peddled white lightning in our community for over two decades, and never, in anyone's memory, spent a day in jail or put out one red cent in fines. Perhaps Old Fent's ways were those of an outcast, a man harrassed continually by the law, snubbed by proper folks, and harangued in absentia by preachers of all denominations.

Fent was the very soul of caution, so much so that staying out of trouble was with him a kind of game. He never retailed any white moon himself, finding it a lot safer to unload the produce of his still through a string of penny-ante sellers. Once a traveling salesman stopped in Millerville and asked the loafers at Cook's blacksmith shop if they could put him onto a pint of good white likker. They sent him to see Fent Newsome, and that proved to be acutely embarrassing to the hapless fellow. Fent cussed the surprised stranger out, and reminded him that he was in the presence of a Christian gentleman who'd have nothing to do with such filthy business. Had the traveling man stuck around for a day or two more, someone might have taken him down to the Ogeechee bottoms to watch Fent haul out a load of panther sweat to slake the local citizens' weekend thirsts.

Deacon Josh Wiggins couldn't abide the thought of any kind of devilment going on around our community, and being comfortably well off, he could afford to pay a small army of informers to keep him up on all of the local dirt. Some of Deacon Josh's spies doubled as retailers for Fent Newsome, so Sheriff Barnwell Tate could never be sure whether the information the good deacon passed along would lead him to, or away from, Fent's operations. Even if Sheriff Tate did get lucky and set a stakeout in the right place, a remarkable gift of Pender Jane's helped her owner slip through uncaught. That old gray plug could sniff out the law from as much as half a mile away.

Tooky Calhoun, who helped around Fent's still, described the old mule's talents to the loafers at Cook's blacksmith shop one Saturday afternoon when I happened to be hanging around. Old Jane might be joggling along some trail in the Ogeechee bottoms with Fent half asleep on the wagon seat, when her normally floppy ears would prick forward suddenly. She'd raise her head and gaze about, first to the left and then to the right. Then she'd commence snorting in that harsh rattle that tells you a mule is upset, and if Fent didn't rein her up promptly, she would slow down gradually and finally come to a dead halt.

If Fent happened to be in a hurry, he'd just gee his mule around and take an alternate route to the rendezvous with his retailers. If, on the other hand, he was in no hurry and felt in a devilish mood, he might stash his cargo in a thicket, calm Old Jane, and ride on up to Sheriff Tate's stakeout as nonchalantly as you please. While Wilbur Godbee, Sheriff Tate's deputy, searched the wagon, Fent would pass the time of day with the Sheriff, inquiring as to the lawman's health and that of his family. Old Fent could be right civil on those occasions, tipping his hat when he finally drove off, and never snickering until he was out of sight down the road.

The closest Fent ever came to getting caught with his overalls at half-mast was one foggy morning in the fall of 1935. The Sunday before, one of Deacon Josh Wiggins' spies learned the whereabouts of Fent's still and lost no time passing the information on to his employer, who just as quickly relayed it to Sheriff Tate. The next morning Sheriff Tate and Deputy Godbee drove their prowl car, a 1929 Dodge, into the Ogeechee Swamp, hoping to sniff out Fent's still before the wily moonshiner got wind of what they were up to.

The old Dodge made fair time sloshing its way along the corduroy logging road pointed out by Deacon Josh's informer, who rode along in the back seat. For once Sheriff Tate believed that he had Fent Newsome fair bottled up. With any luck at all, they'd nab him with his still a-thumping. If not, they'd be able to put him out of business, if only temporarily.

What the Sheriff did not know was that Fent Newsome was up ahead on the crude road with enough sugar and cornmeal on his wagon to run off fifty gallons of prime panther sweat. Fent, however, knew that the law was on his tail because Pender Jane had sounded the alarm minutes before her beleaguered master finally heard the prowl car whining its way ever closer to his new copper-pot still.

Fent Newsome was a realist. He knew blamed well that if

he wished to remain a free man he had to keep out of Sheriff Tate's sight. Being caught on the way to one's still was, in the absence of sympathetic witnesses, the same as being nabbed at the still. He had to find a way to thwart the law, and find it in a quick hurry.

A hundred yards ahead lay a pole bridge spanning a stagnant creek some twenty yards wide. Fent drove across, took an ax, and went to work on the sleepers beneath the bridge. A few chops, and the half-rotten stringers were ready to collapse under their own weight.

Fent barely had time enough to slog ashore and whip Old Jane into her best jog before the prowl car creaked around a bend and rolled confidently onto the bridge. As the bootlegger told it later, he'd just pulled off into a canebrake when he heard the bridge snap. There was a loud crack, followed by a big splash, a streak of cussing, and then silence.

Sheriff Tate's party showed up in Millerville near noon, muddy and on foot. They hired Mincey's garage to send in a wrecker to snake the Dodge out, and that was the last anyone ever heard of the incident from Sheriff Tate's lips. To this day, I don't know whether or not they found Fent's still.

If Fent Newsome and his mule were unlike in so many ways, they still complemented each other in some of their differences. One of the most curious contrasts between the pair concerned their respective attitudes toward strong drink. Although Fent was devoted to making and selling scorpion juice, he wouldn't touch it otherwise, probably because he was so well acquainted with what went into it. Pender Jane, on the other hand, was virtually a souse, having come by her craving from swilling on the worked-out slops from Fent's still. Widespread knowledge of the old plug's bizarre taste was bound to lead, sooner or later, to someone's playing an equally bizarre joke on her. The moment of destiny arrived, so to speak, one warm Saturday afternoon in Mr. Dawse Cook's blacksmith shop.

The market-day loafers were sitting around slapping at flies and hashing over Fent's latest scrape with the law, when Mr. Fate Evans showed up rolling a forty-gallon vinegar barrel. The attention of all was immediately riveted on the barrel and the reasons why Mr. Fate might be rolling it around. The storekeeper explained that he had just finished draining the barrel, and was about to store it in his warehouse, when it occurred to him that it would make a splendid vessel for brewing a batch of cornbuck. By some telepathic process all the people present, including me, knew immediately just what the merchant had in mind.

Mr. Dawse Cook was never one to stand around idle when there was important work to be done. First he sent me over to the grist mill next door with a note for the miller, Coot Mixon, to bring over six pecks of cracked corn, the stuff we called scratch feed. That done, he dispatched Mr. Clyde Tilley and Rufus Catoe over to Evans' General Store to fetch three gallons of blackstrap molasses and a packet of brewer's yeast.

Naturally everybody wanted to help with the cornbuck, so Mr. Dawse had us line up and take turns with the mixing and the stirring. I was next to last in line and got to dump in the yeast. After all had had a chance to make a contribution of labor or advice, Mr. Dawse capped the barrel with several folds of cheesecloth tied down with baling wire. Mr. Dawse explained that he'd covered the barrel to keep out flies and yellow jackets, but most believed that it was to keep his cronies from drinking the barrel empty before Pender Jane got the chance.

By late Sunday morning the cornbuck was working nicely,

frothing and bubbling and giving off a heady aroma that wafted over town and up to the First Baptist Church, where Deacon Josh Wiggins was prompted to say that he'd be dinged if it didn't smell like Fent Newsome had finally moved his still to town.

A week passed, and Fent Newsome, as was his Saturday custom, arrived in town at two o'clock sharp. After looping Pender Jane's reins around a hitching post in front of the smithy, the moonshiner scowled at the small crowd gathered nearby and went off to see after his retailers.

As soon as Fent was out of sight good, Mr. Cook dipped up a half-bushel foot tub of the cornbuck and offered it to old Jane. Like most mules who've endured a long life of patient toil, Pender Jane dropped her head and dozed off whenever an opportunity presented. But when she got a whiff of that rich, heady cornbuck coming her way, she perked up and brayed like a young jackass on the prod.

The old mule gulped down the first tubful without raising her head. She dispatched the second almost as fast, and was near the bottom of her third when she began to shift unsteadily on her feet. Mr. Dawse had slipped me a dime to act as a lookout. I stood a block away with my eyes on Fails' Cafe, where Fent transacted most of his business. My neck fair ached from switching my gaze from the cafe to Pender Jane, I was that concerned that I might miss something.

I shifted my eyes back just in time to see Pender Jane's legs buckle. Mr. Clyde Tilley had been leaning against her withers, affectionately loaded in his own right. He had tried to prop the old mule up, but finally had had to step back smartly to keep from being pinned beneath her when she fell. Once down, old Jane didn't thrash about, or try to get up, or even move.

She just lay stretched out in front of the blacksmith shop in inebriated contentment, a smile on her long face, or so it appeared to me.

The better part of an hour passed before Fent returned. By then a sizable crowd had gathered around the prostrate mule. When those on the fringe smiled at Fent in a knowing way, all of the moonshiner's instincts for sensing trouble shifted into gear. He elbowed his way through the crowd and kicked Pender Jane on the rump, demanding that she get up and quit cuttin' the fool. Her only response was a thunderous fart, followed by a feeble switch of her tail. Then somebody whispered, loud enough for Fent to hear, that the old plug looked foundered. On hearing that, Fent got alarmed and went in search of Swint Fuller, who happened to be in town looking after some puny mules over at Parker's Livery Stable.

Old Doc Swint arrived in due time, and immediately set about making his diagnosis. He thumped Old Jane on the belly with the heel of his hand while listening intently to the rumblings within. After a minute or two of tapping and listening, Doc Fuller shook his head and allowed that the patient's belly sounded too loose to indicate gravel, but, since her paunch was obviously tight, it wouldn't hurt to purge her out with calomel or linseed oil. Pressure over the kidneys produced no reaction, so cramp colic was ruled out.

After more puttering and fidgeting, Old Swint scratched his head in bewilderment. Then, as a sort of last resort, he went to his veterinary satchel, got out a mouth stretcher, and while Fent held his mule's head steady, the old horse doctor prized her mouth open and looked in. Her breath danged near knocked him flat.

Old Doc Swint got to his feet, grinned, and sniffed deeply

of the moist evening air. Striking a hot trail, Doc Fuller followed his nose directly into the smithy. He wasn't the only one that came close to fainting when we saw how much of the barrel's contents was missing. Doc Swint advised Fent to ice down Pender Jane's legs, or if he could get her to her feet, to stand her in a branch overnight, because in the doctor's studied opinion, it would be a stomped-down wonder if the patient didn't come down with founder. That done, Swint Fuller gathered up the tools of his profession and departed without even asking for a fee. I suppose he felt that just being in on the prank, even if belatedly, had been compensation enough.

Speaking for all of us, Mr. Dawse apologized to Fent for having gotten his mule stoned to the point of founder. We hadn't expected her to drink so much. We'd intended no harm, but when we saw how eagerly she'd lapped up the cornbuck, we'd just naturally gotten carried away. Anyway, things weren't quite as bad as they looked. About half of the cornbuck had actually been swilled up by the crowd. Mr. Cook offered to replace free of charge a wagon shaft broken in Old Jane's fall, and further offered to take up a collection to pay for the mule in case she didn't come around.

Fent couldn't see a blamed bit of humor in our getting his mule loaded. He didn't want any apologies, or anything else, from such a lowdown bunch. He proceeded to cuss us out, and before anyone could move, he'd whipped out a switchblade knife and made for the blacksmith, declaring that he would cut the sonofabitch's guts out if it was the last thing he ever did.

Old Fent might have sliced Mr. Cook up real bad if someone hadn't had the presence of mind to toss the blacksmith a five-pound sledge. That evened the scrap up until Constable Lange arrived with Sheriff Barnwell Tate. Mr. Cook was more than happy to settle for a draw, but Sheriff Tate had to pull his revolver on Fent before that tough moonshiner would put his knife away.

I was pretty unnerved by the time the law arrived, so I took my dime over to Evans' General Store and found gratification in an RC Cola and a sack of grab-bag candy. Around dusk I slipped back over to the blacksmith shop to check on Pender Jane's progress. I found her on her feet but still wobbly. Mr. Cook had already replaced the broken wagon shaft so that by good dark the old gray mule was able to stagger home.

We didn't see much of Pender Jane around Millerville after that particular Saturday. Fent bought a secondhand pickup truck and took to driving it to town. He continued to use his old gray plug in his moonshining operations, however. After all, pickup trucks are noisy and hard on swamp bridges, and I've not seen one yet that could sniff out the law. Occasionally thereafter my pals and I ran into Fent and his mule on back-woods trails. Pender Jane always ignored us, but Fent never failed to give us a look that chilled us to the marrow.

Eventually old Pender Jane just faded from the scene, passing either from age or from the effects of one last glorious toot at Fent's mash barrels. I would like to think that she is up in those Elysian pastures where good mules go, standing knee-deep in clover and munching on bright new oats. Wherever she may be, in paradise or otherwise, I hope there are tubs of sweet, rich cornbuck for her to sip on when she's bored. After all, if men and mules must while away all eternity, they should be allowed to do it in a style befitting their most singular attributes.

MINNIE AND ALICE

MUCH WORK performed by mules in Grand-father's and Daddy's time required team effort. In fact, tasks like siding cotton with a riding cultivator required a degree of intrateam coordination characteristic of mated mules, pairs that often worked together like the cogs of a finely tuned watch. Not surprisingly, people fortunate enough to own such mules prized them greatly, so much so that a mated team frequently brought more on the market than could be realized from selling the mules separately.

Although some mules became mates long after they had departed the green pastures of their colthood days, most were animals that had grown up together, sharing each other's company and thus developing emotional ties that often seemed more human than mulelike. Minnie and Alice, a splendid pair that belonged to my daddy during the late 1930s, seemed to have come by their attachment in that way.

Daddy first heard of the mules through a neighbor, Mr. Clay Parker. Mr. Parker had just returned from Dover, the county seat, where he'd seen a fine-looking pair of young mules at Cribbens and Foxhall's stables. He'd wanted to buy the smaller of the pair, Alice, but Mr. Cribbens hadn't wanted to separate the mules. Knowing that Daddy was in the market for a new team, Mr. Parker urged him to look Minnie and Alice over before making any firm commitments.

The next day Daddy, Uncle Lester, and Deacon Andrew Tolbert drove over to check the mules out. Uncle Lester took an immediate liking to Alice, admiring her clean limbs, upright carriage, and alert looks. He found her colors, soft dun with chocolate mane and tail, a little unusual, but a shrewd buyer never judged a mule by its color. At around 1100 pounds, Alice was a good 400 pounds lighter than her mate, Minnie. Minnie's colors were more usual for a mule, dark bay with a black saddle over her flanks.

Uncle Lester had some reservations about Minnie. She was, like Alice, a clean-limbed, stylish mule, but she seemed inclined to get upset if anyone got between her and her mate. However, Uncle Lester pointed out that he was along only to render an opinion and not to make the final judgment. That was up to Daddy. Daddy studied for a moment and offered the final say-so to Deacon Andrew Tolbert, who, along with his son C. T., would be working the mules. Daddy pointed out that they would have to put up with any bad habits the pair might have. Deacon Tolbert nodded and said he was confident that he could work with Minnie, even if she was a little skitterish, and he saw no reason why his son should have any trouble with Alice. That decided, Daddy signed a $350 note for the pair, and they were delivered to our place the next day.

The two hadn't been with us long before it became obvious that Alice was a very crafty sort of mule, one inclined to mischief. Minnie, on the other hand, proved to be steady and obedient, if not overly bright. She behaved well and turned out a full day's work, provided she wasn't separated from her mate. Deacon Andrew Tolbert discovered that fact about Minnie in a most convincing way one Saturday morning in April, 1938, scarcely a month after Daddy had bought the pair.

Among Daddy's holdings was a thirty-acre field across Simmons Branch from our farmstead. The lower end of the field was the kind of land called light pond bottom and was planted in sugar cane. At the time, Daddy and his croppers grew about seven acres of cane per year, enough to make several barrels of high-quality syrup for home use and for the local markets. That particular morning Deacon Tolbert hitched Minnie to a Jersey wagon and drove across the branch to throw beds to his newly sprouted cane stubble. Later the Deacon told us he'd noticed that Minnie had been a little nervous when they were ready to leave, but he'd thought little of her anxiety at the time.

The plowing commenced smoothly enough until the Deacon tied Minnie to a fence post and went down to the springhead to get a drink of water. When he got back, Minnie was missing, although her tracks where she'd broken loose and fled were plain enough. Judging from the trail she'd left, Minnie had raced helter-skelter about the field before finally leaping over the fence near a thicket. Deacon Tolbert tracked her for a ways into the tangle only to have her trail peter out in a growth of gum scrubs and bamboo briers.

Daddy stopped by the field just as Deacon Tolbert was about to return home to report Minnie's escape. Daddy was all for having me and Ceroy Tolbert, the Deacon's younger son, scour the branch woods for signs of Minnie's trail, but Deacon Tolbert demurred.

"Jimmy, if them boys was to come up on that mule sudden-like with her lost and scared, she might not stop this side of Jenkins County. C. T.'s back yonder behind the barn with Alice, throwin' out corn middles. Why don't we have him ride Alice back into them woods? When Minnie smells her mate, she's bound to come on out."

C. T. Tolbert took Alice out and rode her into the branch woods near the spot where his father had lost Minnie's trail. After wandering about for a short while, Alice lifted her head and brayed softly. Minnie came crashing out of a ty-ty thicket, bug-eyed with fear and rattling in her throat. She snuggled up so close to Alice she almost pushed C. T. from his seat. Needless to say, she was happy to follow her mate home.

A week passed before Minnie had settled down enough to go back to work. Then and there Daddy decided that she was not to be worked out of sight of her mate again. With that precaution, Minnie became one of the steadiest and most dependable mules I've ever had the pleasure to work with.

Teaming Alice up with C. T. didn't work out at all. That jarhead was so mischievous and sly the youth couldn't keep up with her. If he let her reins go slack for a split second, she was likely to bite the top out of a particularly tall hill of corn or wander off the row to crop a choice tuft of crabgrass. Sometimes she'd step over the drill into the next middle, leaving C. T. to wonder why he was walking down the opposite row. Once Deacon Tolbert tried curbing her appetite by fitting her with a wire muzzle, but Alice quickly learned to shuck the muzzle by rubbing it loose on her foreleg. Then, freed of the aggravating contraption, she'd go on topping corn, cotton, and even tobacco, the only mule I ever saw that would touch the weed.

Unlike most mules, Alice seemed to have an acute sense of time. As noon approached, she'd commence staring off in the direction of the bell post near the corner of our kitchen. She'd bray as though urging the bell to ring. When it finally rang, she'd stop, whether in the middle of a row or at the end of one, and C. T. would have to take her out where she stood. Mama usually had one of us kids ring the bell, and if we happened to delay ringing it for as little as five minutes, Alice was likely to take off for the barn lot anyway, dragging plow and, if need be, plow hand behind her. Luckily for me, my parents never learned that I delayed ringing the bell more than once just to watch Alice cut up, or they would have skinned me alive. Minnie, on the other hand, would have worked through the noon hour and on into the night, provided of course that Alice was nearby.

Finally Deacon Tolbert had to admit that his son simply couldn't handle Alice. In fact, some of the wage hands whispered, behind C. T.'s back, that Old Alice had more natural-born gumption than the Deacon's older son. The Deacon turned Minnie over to C. T. and set about trying to straighten Alice out himself. Under his firm hand, her deportment improved markedly.

The relationship between Minnie and Alice was odd, even for mules. Most mated mules share a mutual attraction, and so it was with our pair. However, Alice was the more independent of the two. She would work with other mules, provided she could work on the side of the team that she preferred. Minnie would perform in double harness only with her mate, and of course worked well in single harness only if Alice was nearby. C. T. Tolbert told me once that when he and Minnie were siding long cotton rows, Minnie would hold up at the ends and peer about until she spotted Alice. It was as if she couldn't recall that her mate was working in the same field and wasn't reassured until she got a good look at her. Such behavior confirmed our earlier suspicions that Minnie, though a top quality mule, was nonetheless not a very bright one, and was utterly dependent upon her mate for emotional support.

One of Alice's most aggravating traits was an ability to jump fences like an Irish hunter. That, along with a hatred for cows that amounted to a desire to commit murder, got her into trouble more than once. I well remember the morning she tangled with Deacon Josh Wiggins' bull.

69

Deacon Josh ran a small dairy at the time, and kept a pedigreed Guernsey bull for upgrading his milch stock. The Guernsey, like many another bull then and now, was hard to keep put. He broke out of his pen regularly and wandered off to check up on the neighbors' cows. One Saturday morning just as we had finished milking, the bull showed up at the cow-pen gate and stood peering through the slats waiting for us to turn the milch cows out for the day's grazing. Over in the barn lot Alice spotted the bull, and before anyone could make a move to stop her, she jumped the lot fence and made for the Guernsey with her teeth bared.

Ordinarily Deacon Josh's Guernsey was tolerably docile, but when he saw that mule racing at him with mayhem in her heart, he turned and charged her without so much as a preliminary howdy-do. The pair scuffled back and forth for a few moments while I watched with my heart in my throat. Alice bit and slashed at the bull's withers, while the Guernsey nudged at her belly with his burly head. Slowly but surely the powerful animal shoved Alice toward the lot fence. Once he had her fair pinned, Deacon Josh's bull flipped Alice over his back as easily as a bluetick hound tosses a coon. Then, being a gentlemanly sort, the bull turned and walked casually away. Luckily the Guernsey was butt-headed, or we might have lost a good mule that morning.

About a year later one of our milch cows, Old Sissy Belle, came close to finishing Alice for good. Ordinarily Sissy Belle was about as gentle as the average run of bossies, but when she had a new calf at her side she could be touchy and unpredictable. Then, out of respect for her uncertain temper and wicked, upcurved horns, we were content to leave her be.

If Alice was aware of the dangers in tampering with the old cow at maternity time, she didn't show it that spring morning in 1940. The night before, Sissy Belle had given birth to a sturdy bull calf, her twelfth, according to Mama's reckoning. Alice couldn't abide the sight of that new calf. She spent the morning pacing up and down along the barn-lot fence, glaring over into the cowpen. Just before noon she backed off, took a running start, and sailed over the fence, clearing by a good six inches a strand of barbed wire Daddy had strung along the top of the fence especially to keep her put.

Alice had scarcely landed before Sissy Belle was under her, ripping and tearing at her belly with those deadly horns. That old cow was in a fair way of goring Alice to death when Daddy rushed out and drove her off with a pitchfork at considerable risk to his own skin.

Alice was a mighty sick mule when Dr. Lewis Wilding arrived about an hour later to patch her up. He disinfected her wounds, sewed up three gaping holes in her belly, and rigged up a sling for her to recuperate in. It was touch and go for about a week, but Alice had more than her share of bottom. Within a month she was up and around, scarred but not altogether contrite. She would still take off after any cow that crossed her path—any, that is, except Old Sissy Belle. From the day of her goring, Alice gave those murderous horns a wide berth.

When I left for the war in 1942, Minnie and Alice were pulling more than their share of weight around the farm. When I returned home in 1946, they were not there. I didn't ask Daddy where they'd gone, knowing that some of the decisions that must be made around a farm are neither easy nor pleasant to talk about afterwards. One bright morning that June, Daddy and I drifted down the Ogeechee, pitching catalpa worms after redbreast and bream. During a lull in the fishing, Daddy told me of Minnie's and Alice's fate.

71

The winter before I was mustered out, Minnie had stumbled over the doorsill of her stable, straining her left stifle joint in the process. The injury had not responded to treatment, and by early spring it had become obvious that Minnie was crippled for good. Needing a mule to start the spring crop, Daddy had had no alternative but to replace her. My father didn't reveal who'd taken Minnie off his hands, but I suspected that it had been one Pegleg Cleland, an itinerant jobber who bought mostly "killers" for the pet food trade.

I asked Daddy why he'd had to let Alice go. He told me that she'd become unmanageable once her mate had gone. She had refused to work and had spent most of her time breaking out of the barnlot and running off in search of Minnie. I'd always believed that the hellion was an independent jarhead, one that didn't much care if the sun set or rose, as long as she got her daily hay and oats and the chance to chase a calf now and then. Evidently I was wrong. Alice's affection for Minnie, though it didn't always show, was about as strong as Minnie's had been for Alice. That pair had formed an attachment that seemed altogether more human than mulelike, and the death of one was a shattering experience for the other.

HATTIE AND MATTIE,
THE BLUE-NOSED MULES

INNIE and Alice were about as devoted to each other as any pair of mules could be, yet curiously, there was little about the two to suggest that they were in any way kin. For example, Minnie was much larger than her mate, and the mules' colors were very different. Some other pairs of mated mules were matched; that is, they were of the same colors, size, and sex, and were often closely related. Daddy told me once of a pair of iron-gray mules owned by Grandfather when Daddy was a lad. That particular pair of mules had been full sisters, and the two had performed to perfection when working together. I knew of a few pairs of matched mules in my Millerville days, but most of those were rather ordinary jarheads, good workers but otherwise rather colorless. Certainly none of those matched pairs of my acquaintance came anywhere near Old Hattie and Mattie, the blue-nosed mules, in pure character.

I suspect that many might find the term *blue-nosed* startling when applied to mules; doubtless it conjures up visions of jarheads with bright turquoise snouts. Unfortunately, that is not the case. The blue-nosed kind had ordinary black noses like most hardtails. What made blue-nosed mules special was their pattern of colors. Besides ordinary bay, gray, and various shades of black and brownish-black with white trimmings, there existed mules that were coal-black all over, and those were known as blue-nosed. That pattern was unusual because most dark-colored mules had white markings on the muzzle, around the eyes, or even on the belly. Those white markings are rare in horses, but are of virtually universal occurrence in asses. Moreover, the white points of asses bred strong in crossing with horses. Presumably there must have been blue-nosed jackasses around, though I never saw one. I can't imagine how else mules like Hattie and Mattie came by their blue noses.

I never knew the mules personally, since they had come along before my time, so I shall tell their story approximately as the Old Cap'n told it to Mr. Fate Evans and me. I heard about Hattie and Mattie as a result of an argument between Mr. Fate and the Old Cap'n over whether or not a mule's color had anything to do with its disposition. Mr. Fate believed, like most at the time, that a blue-nosed mule was invariably stubborn, whereas Grandfather insisted that a mule's color had nothing to do with what went on under its skin, unless of course the owner happened to be prejudiced against a certain color and took out his rancor on the poor brute with the offending hue. To support his contention, Grandfather offered the story of Hattie and Mattie. I must admit to coming away bewildered, for, the Old Cap'n's word notwithstanding, those jarheads did sound a bit stubborn to me.

Old Hattie and Mattie were a perfectly matched pair, very likely full sisters just a year apart in age. They earned their daily hay and oats toiling at the Parker and Millhouse brick factory near Millerville in the 1920s. Their task was pulling a clay cart from pits about a half-mile from the factory to a vat where the raw clay was moistened and kneaded before being molded into bricks. That particular cart looked like a chopped-down railway hopper car, the kind used for hauling coal. Like a coal car, the clay cart had a trapdoor at its bottom through which the clay was dumped.

On weekday mornings Coot Mixon, a rangy fellow then Hattie and Mattie's driver, showed up at the mill at 7:45 A.M. sharp, hitched Hattie and Mattie to the clay cart, and hauled brick clay until the noon whistle blew. Hattie and Mattie, like the other mill hands, knocked off for dinner, and like their human counterparts, they quit where the noon whistle caught them. It made no difference to that pair if the cart was within ten feet of the vat with a load of clay. When that noon whistle sounded, they stopped, and Coot had to take them out then and there. When the whistle blew for the resumption of work at one o'clock, they were willing to pull the cart the remaining distance to the vat, but not one second before.

Coot was meticulous about his work. It stung his sense of propriety to have to leave a load of clay sitting within feet of the vat undumped. Moreover, if left too long in the cart, damp clay had a tendency to pack down so that Coot might have to prize it out with a shovel. Once he talked Sim Flinoy, who fired the mill's boiler, into watching out for him as noon approached. If Coot happened to be within sight of the mill with a load, Sim was to hold off pulling the whistle until the cart had been dumped. That dodge fooled Hattie and Mattie, but it didn't fool their human counterparts for long. They raised Holy Ned and threatened to tar and feather poor Sim if he didn't go back to the regularly observed schedule.

There was another team of mules at the brick factory besides Hattie and Mattie. Grandfather couldn't recall much about them except that their task was hauling wood to fuel the brick kilns. One morning one of the wood-wagon mules came down with a strained stifle joint. Frequently when a mule's stifle joint is overstretched, the lower end of the hipbone pops out of place. Swint Fuller set stifle joints by looping a rope around the hock of the affected member and then tying the other end of the rope to a stout post. The mule was then led away to stretch the hipbone back into place. After resetting a stifle joint, Old Doc Fuller might blister the point of the hip with Gombault's Caustic Balsam to draw blood to the injury and promote healing. After these drastic measures, the afflicted mule was frequently out of work for several days.

Brick sales were uncommonly brisk at the time of the mule's injury, so it wasn't long before the kiln crew ran short on fuel. Coot tried hitching Hattie and Mattie to the wood wagon to fetch a few loads of cordwood, but that pair refused to budge with the unfamiliar vehicle. The only way Coot could get his team to haul wood was to go after it in the clay cart. That worked out well enough until the noon whistle caught Coot and his team on the public road about a mile from the mill. Hattie and Mattie refused to go further, even to move the cart over to the road's shoulder. After that hassle, Mr. Millhouse rented a mule from Parker's Livery Stable and put Hattie and Mattie back to hauling clay.

Brick sales were so bullish in 1927 that Mr. Millhouse decided to have an additional kiln built. A black masonry contractor named Young Willie Rilington was hired to do the work. Grandfather recalled that Young Willie was a skilled workman who could lay bricks and mortar just about as fast as two helpers could supply the makings.

Heavy rains that July threw Young Willie and his crew behind, so they started working nights to catch up. In order to further speed the work, Young Willie hired Coot to help out after regular hours toting bricks and mixing mortar.

One sultry evening in late July, Coot stood at the clay vat mixing a batch of mortar in the clay cart. After the mortar had been stirred well, Coot planned to haul it to the kiln site and dump it into a pit for use over the weekend. Puddled mortar, if covered well, will remain usable for days in a pit.

While Coot stirred the fresh mortar with a grubbing hoe, Hattie and Mattie stood placidly to the cart, staring off into the gathering dusk as if it were the beginning of a regular workday. Unlike Daddy's Alice, that pair seemed to have little sense of the passage of time. If fed, watered, and allowed to rest for a spell, they were ready to resume work, day or night, provided of course no one blew the mill whistle on them.

That same evening Sam Catoe slipped his boat away from its mooring beneath the Ogeechee River bridge and headed downriver toward Lee's Landing. Some of Sam's cronies were at the landing fishing for cats and eels; that is, they were drowning worms while simultaneously drowning their cares in a jug of Fent Newsome's white lightning.

Sam had plans for serenading them with his whangdoodle, an instrument made from a polished goatskin stretched over one end of a section sawn from a hollow cypress knee. A length of trotline cord was attached to the tympanic head of the whangdoodle through its body. When well rosined and plucked with a scrap of felt, the cord gave off a caterwaul that sounded somewhere between the squall of an infuriated panther and the bleat of a dying calf in a hailstorm.

Coot had just parked the cart by the kiln when the first raucus snarls of the whangdoodle drifted over the swamp. There is no record of how Sam's buddies reacted to his whangdoodling, but when the first notes tore through the air surrounding the brick kilns, they struck mortal terror into the hearts of Coot Mixon and the masonry crew. Young Willie and his helpers took refuge in a metal stack lying on the ground by the unfinished kiln. Coot tried to squeeze in with them, but there was no room left. Finding no other suitable place to hide, Coot proceeded to light a shuck for home.

77

Coot lived two miles away in Fork Field, a swampy neck of land jammed in between the Ogeechee River and Big Horse Creek. According to Young Willie, Coot took off for home yelling for his wife Nellie to open the door. Old Coot must have made right good time pounding his way through the bog holes and palmetto thickets of the creek swamp, judging from the trail he left. Somehow he got off the road leading to his house and missed the bridge over Horse Creek, but that didn't slow him down in the least. Coot cleared the creek without wetting a heel, a prodigious leap of some twenty-two feet. Nellie didn't hear Coot coming until he was already on the front steps. Before the poor woman could get the door open, Coot knocked it off its hinges and was cowering under the bedcovers before his surprised wife could ask him if he'd taken leave of his senses.

An hour passed before Young Willie and his helpers mustered the courage to emerge from the stack. They found Hattie and Mattie where Coot had left them, blinking in the darkness and doubtless wondering just what all the commotion had been about. To the immense relief of his helpers, Young Willie drove the mules back to their stable and knocked off for the night.

I would have liked to hear more about Hattie and Mattie and their life and times, but other matters were pressing for Grandfather, so the story was ended for the day. A few days later I asked him to take up where he'd left off, but he mentioned only that Hattie and Mattie had been auctioned off with the mill's assets when the firm went bankrupt in 1929. He'd wanted the mules, but arrived at the auction just as they were being led away by a farmer from over in Buford County. I've often wondered what that farmer thought when his new team refused to work with anything but a clay cart.

When I was a pupil at the Millerville Grammar School, our class liked to hold outings at the brickyard site. We kids spent many a happy hour climbing over the abandoned kilns and playing fox and hounds in the clay pits. A few years back a Mr. Harrington bought the property with the intent of turning it into a fishing club. The ruined buildings were cleared away to make room for a clubhouse, and the outlets from the clay pits dammed to make some impressive-sized ponds. One warm night last June I stopped off at the Brickyard Club to listen to the cowbell frogs sing in the bonnet lilies that now cover the ponds. As those little green frogs yammered out their strident "wa-a-a-nk! wa-a-a-nk!" I conjured up a vision of Old Coot whooping and whistling, urging Hattie and Mattie in before the noon whistle sounded.

I have often suspected that Grandfather may have been wrong about Hattie and Mattie. Those jarheads were stubborn, but not because of their colors. Like anyone with any self-respect, they got their dander up when they felt that their entitles were being infringed upon. In that way mules can be a lot like humans. Respect a mule's rights and you'll get along with it well enough, whether its nose is aquamarine or just plain black.

COOT MIXON'S BRUSH
WITH THE LAW

DURING my boyhood days most of the rural citizens around Millerville were hardworking folks who stayed straight and sober through the week. Saturdays, however, were likely to be a different matter. Just about everybody—men, women, and children—showed up in town on market days, and there were many who couldn't stand the strain of town-life sociability for more than a few hours at a stretch. For those, there was always plenty of raw moonshine around to allay such tensions as might develop.

As Deacon Josh Wiggins was fond of saying, Mr. Clyde Tilley was one of the worst of those dinged Saturday night drunks. Coot Mixon was another. When I knew Coot, the brick factory where he had once worked was in ruins, but he and his wife Nellie still dwelt on their little farm in Fork Field. They farmed their soggy acres, and Coot eked out their existence running a grist mill on Saturdays for Mr. Dawse Cook, the blacksmith. Most Saturdays Coot arrived in town around one o'clock, opened up the mill house, and ground corn for the local citizens until dark. Then, after sacking the day's tolls, he dusted off his overalls, locked the mill, and joined his cronies at Fails' Cafe.

From outward appearances, Fails' Cafe was an eating joint, featuring catfish sandwiches. However, Deacon Josh Wiggins claimed that the dinged place would have gone bankrupt on what Lige Fails cleared dishing up fried fish on stale light-bread. In actual fact, Lige ran the cafe as a front for retailing Fent Newsome's white lightning, sold either by the drink or by the bottle.

Although my parents wouldn't allow me near the place, I heard from various sources that there were two rooms off to one side that Lige used for living quarters, a room in the back with two decrepit pool tables, and a larger room in the front with a counter for serving food and drink. Bottled stock was kept stashed in a pine thicket out back, with a small black lad serving as fetcher. Likker by the drink was served from a water bucket at one end of the counter. Nearby was a sink into which the contents of the bucket could be poured should the law, or any other unwelcome citizen, show up in the door. Sam Catoe told it around that Lige kept another bucket under the floor beneath the sink to catch any moon that had to be scuttled. The nether bucket could be retrieved, once the coast was clear, through a camouflaged crawl space.

There were times when Coot lasted to midnight before he passed out. Whenever Coot finally slumped to the floor, those of his cronies still able to help laid him in his wagon, gave his mule, Ficey Ann, her head, and pointed her in the direction for home. Old Ficey Ann was one of the smallest mules I ever saw. I don't believe she would have topped 700 pounds wringing wet. Yet at least half of that little jarhead's bulk must have been pure heart, because she never failed to negotiate the trail to Coot's house in fair weather and foul, through pitch darkness and driving rain. She had to cross a bridge over Big Horse Creek that was barely wide enough to accommodate the wagon's wheels. Still, as far as anyone knew, she never once strayed from her accustomed path, nor did she ever have a mishap while negotiating that narrow bridge.

Once home, Ficey Ann, like Mr. Clyde's Bill, would stand

braying by the yard gate until Nellie got up and took her out. Understandably, Mrs. Mixon was never very anxious to answer the mule's call. There were times when Coot's beleaguered wife just buried her head beneath the pillow and let the poor animal bray. Fork Field swarmed with mosquitoes during warm weather, so there must have been times when those swamp gallernippers went off on toots of their own from sucking up Coot's high-proof gore.

One Sunday morning in the fall of 1936, Mayor Jim Skinner had just risen from the breakfast table when Nellie Mixon showed up at his kitchen door out of breath and wailing like one possessed. Naturally, Mr. Jim invited the distraught woman in and inquired as to what was ailing her.

"Mr. Jim, I don't know what we're goin' to do. Last night Coot got home around midnight, like he always does on Saturdays. I get so tired of gettin' up and helpin' him to bed with him dog drunk. I rolled over and tried to go back to sleep, but that pore mule kept on brayin'. I come close to faintin' when I saw that bale of cotton on his wagon. I'd of come sooner, but I'm scared to go through that creek swamp at night, and Coot wasn't in no shape to come hisself. Mr. Jim, he must of stole that bale off somebody, but I swanee I can't see how."

Mr. Jim shook his head in disbelief. "Now hold on, Nellie. I don't like to dispute your word, but I don't see how Coot could load a 500-pound bale of cotton onto his wagon sober, much less drunk. You sure about that bale?"

"I got God as a witness. Somebody must of helped him load it. I was wonderin' if you could round up some help to get it back to whoever it belongs to."

"Well, maybe so, but first I think we ought to go over and see Mr. Stonewall Wilson and find out if he's missin' any cotton from his gin. I expect that gang that hangs around Lige

Fails' place went and put up a fancy job on Coot. Mr. Wilson'll help us straighten this nonsense out if it's his cotton they took."

Mr. Stonewall was incredulous at the thought that anyone would have the gall to steal a bale of cotton from his ginnery platform. Nonetheless, when the three arrived at the gin to check, there was one bale missing. Mr. Wilson proceeded to get hot under the collar.

"By granny, that scoundrel did take my cotton. I'm goin' to call Sheriff Tate and have the thievin' rascal arrested. I aim to break up some of this damned foolishness around here if it's the last thing I ever do."

Neither Mr. Jim's entreaties nor Nellie's tears had any effect on Mr. Stonewall. He unlocked the gin office and called up Sheriff Barnwell Tate at his home near the county seat, demanding that he drive over that very second and arrest Coot Mixon for perpetration of an act of grand larceny.

Sheriff Tate was plenty irked at being called away on a Sunday morning over what looked to him like a joke on Coot Mixon. But Mr. Stonewall packed plenty of political weight on the west side of Ogeechee County, so Sheriff Tate got out his prowl car and took off for Millerville with his neck glowing a little redder than usual.

There was already a crowd gathered around the stolen bale when Sheriff Tate arrived. Just as the lawman pulled up, Coot stumbled out onto the front porch, disheveled and bleary-eyed from the night before. Sheriff Tate regarded the alleged miscreant for a moment and spoke.

"Coot-boy, you just tell me now. What in the failin' hell is goin' on here anyway?"

Coot blinked in the bright autumn sunlight and replied, "I swanee, Sheriff, I just don't know."

"Looky here, Coot. I know damned well you didn't steal that

bale of cotton out there on your wagon. Hell, around midnight last night you couldn't even stand up, much less help load a 500-pound bale of cotton. Who done it, boy?"

"Sheriff, I can't remember nothin' from last night. My pa used to say that if somethin' gets caught in your trap, it's yours. That bale's on my wagon, so I guess I must of stole it. I'm sorry, Mr. Stonewall. I didn't know what I was doin'."

"You hear that, Sheriff? The stinkin' rascal just admitted takin' my cotton. Arrest him. I aim to break up some of this blessed lawlessness that's threatenin' to take over around here if I have to send every last single solitary sorry rascal over here to jail."

"Dammit, Stonewall, just hold your tater. I'll arrest anybody here who needs arrestin'. Just give me a chance to get to the bottom of this nonsense."

Sheriff Tate looked the crowd over and noticed that Tooky Calhoun avoided his eyes.

"You there, Tooky Calhoun. Come over here for a minute."

Tooky Calhoun gazed about in alarm. "Sheriff, I didn't have nothin' to do with it, and that's the pure truth. I don't know nothin' about it."

"Well now, Tooky-boy, I didn't say you had anything to do with it, and that's the pure truth. Course, I don't exactly believe you when you say you don't know nothin' about it, and I think I got a cute little old way of smokin' some facts out of you."

Sheriff Tate thumbed through his wallet and made a big to-do about pulling out a small snapshot, cupping his hands to conceal the printed side.

"Know what I got here, Tooky?"

"Looks like a picture to me."

"You're right about that, Tooky-boy, but that ain't all it is. You remember Saturday a week ago when you took that big demijohn from Fent Newsome at the Simmons Branch bridge?"

Tooky Calhoun paled.

"You stashed that jug under the bridge to pick up after dark. What you and Fent didn't know was that my deputy, Wilbur Godbee, was off in the bushes takin' your picture. Oh, he'd of come out and arrested you both right there, but we both know Old Fent would of busted the jug over a bridge banister. We got your jug, Tooky. It, along with this here little old picture, ought to get you and Fent about six months apiece on the chain gang. Course, I might not make a case against you if you was to tell me what went on over at Lige Fails' last night."

Poor Tooky was almost in tears. "Like I told you before, Sheriff, I didn't have nothin' to do with it. I just watched. Sam Catoe thought it up, and he got Foots Mathis and Slim Griner to help him. I swear, Sheriff, that's the pure truth."

"Yeah, I believe you, Tooky. Them jaspers think they're cute. Say, you over there, Sam and them other two. Don't run off now. I expect me and you funny boys are goin' to take a little trip over to the county jail. Course, if you want to make Mr. Stonewall happy enough to bail you out, you'd better help him load that bale onto his truck before we leave."

"Don't look so put out, Sambo. You all had your fun last night, and now I don't think you have any right to begrudge me and Coot ours. Your little joke scared hell out of Coot, and it's causin' me to be late for my Sunday dinner. I expect I'm goin' to laugh every foot of them twenty-five miles back to the county seat, and I hope Coot laughs too; might help him with his hangover. It's up to Mr. Stonewall to press charges, but since you all work at his gin, I expect he'll be over bright and early Monday mornin' to bail you out. I want you to enjoy your little night in the pokey all the same, though. By the way,

Tooky, you might want to keep this picture for a souvenir."

Tooky clutched the photograph eagerly and was relieved to find that it was just a snapshot of Sheriff Tate and Deputy Godbee standing beside a still they'd just blown.

"Tooky-boy, it wasn't Wilbur Godbee that saw you with Fent. It was one of Deacon Josh Wiggins' informers; I ain't sayin' which. When Wilbur got to the bridge, your demijohn was gone. I expect Jim Bo Wiggins took it, but I can't prove it. He must of heard whoever it was who told his daddy about seein' you and Fent, and beat my deputy to the bridge and swiped your jug. Better luck next time."

The case of the purloined cotton evidently made a lasting impression on Coot. He swore off strong drink and joined the Pentecostal Holiness Church, where he rose rapidly to the post of deacon. I know Coot's reformation made Nellie happy, and Old Ficey Ann must have been equally glad. Coot's staying sober on Saturday nights meant that she got home at a decent hour and was resting in her stable before midnight, no longer forced to pull a wagon through ruts and bogholes with her driver dead to the world behind her on the wagon bed.

UNCLE ALEC'S DAY IN COURT

IN EARLIER TIMES every small town had its yardman, a workman who plowed gardens, hauled off rubbish, and performed such other miscellaneous chores as came to hand. The ancient black gentlemen who plied the trade looked about the same, went about their work in the same deliberate, plodding way, and moved from job to job in the same kind of ramshackle little wagon drawn by an aged plug mule.

Millerville's yardman, Uncle Alec Ziegler, fitted the mold perfectly. He was past eighty when I knew him and was a kind of benign Uncle Tom, a gentle soul who had managed to bridge the chasm between black and white. He might have been a slave in his youth, but no one knew for sure because Uncle Alec was real close-mouthed about his past history, never disputing nor confirming any of the vast body of lore that came to surround him. That was doubtless a canny move on the old man's part, for it was the favored position bestowed by his mystique that afforded him the opportunity for an earned livelihood and the overweening sense of dignity that went with it.

During my youth, people showed more affection for their legendary characters than folks seem to display nowadays. I'll never forget the time the townspeople rallied to Uncle Alec's defense after his mule got him into trouble by blocking traffic in the town square. That seemingly innocent happening led to a confrontation between the mayor and a big-city lawyer.

Mayor Jim Skinner came away with his tail feathers singed, and the incident inadvertently put Millerville, the town whose commerce and dignity the mayor took such pains to uphold, on the map.

In order to understand how an upright citizen like Uncle Alec Ziegler could become enmeshed in the toils of the law, as administered by his honor, Mayor Skinner, one needs to know something about the quirks of his mule, Jayrack. Old Jayrack was much less remarkable than her name. In fact, she looked like the average aged plug, being brownish-black in color, with knock knees, splayed hooves, and most of her ribs showing through her ratty-looking hide. Most of the time the old mule was steady and easygoing like her master, but now and then she'd take a notion to sull up, as folks described it, and when one of those moods struck her, she'd sit down like a dog and wouldn't budge until she was good and ready.

Jayrack might sull up just about anyplace—the middle of the public road, the town streets, in some client's garden, anywhere. Yet her contrary spells rarely lasted long or seemed to bother her owner in the least. Uncle Alec never got mad and whaled her with the reins or frailed her out with an oak scrub, as some would have. He'd just ease down from the wagon seat, shake his head, and trudge home, knowing from previous experience that his mule would get up and follow once she got the urge.

Few of the local citizens took more than passing notice of Uncle Alec's mule when she came down with the contraries. As with many things that happened around home on a more or less routine basis, Jayrack's antics became legends in their own right, to be expected and enjoyed while they lasted. However, as is all too often the case, those aspects of the old plug's behavior that most people found diverting were viewed virtually as anathema by a few others. Deacon Josh Wiggins complained that it was a dinged nuisance having to be forever driving around a mule stalled in the streets, and Mayor Skinner, ever the civic-minded promoter, declared that Uncle Alec and his mule made Millerville look countrified and backward. More than once I heard him caution Uncle Alec to curb his mule or run the risk of having to face the consequences.

I don't remember my home town as being any more backward than any other town its size, but it did look real countrified on Saturdays when rural folks gathered from miles around to swap gossip and trade at the stores. It was like that on one Saturday afternoon in April, 1936, when Old Jayrack decided to sull up right smack in the middle of the town square. Fortunately I needed a theme for an English composition at the time, so I paid particular attention to the happenings that Saturday and to the events that followed.

No one in the market-day crowd seemed at all put out over Jayrack's blocking traffic. Had anyone needed to drive by the spot where she was stalled, all he had to do was cut around on the opposite side of the artesian well, which stood in the center of the square, or else jog over one block. But when Mayor Skinner got the news that the old mule was impeding traffic, he was fit to be tied. He stomped out of the depot, where he worked as railway station agent, and rushed over to the town calaboose to get Constable Lange. Together they tried tugging Jayrack to her feet, but they had no more luck getting her up than Uncle Alec had had. Not being the sort who could tolerate failure, Mayor Skinner rushed back over to the depot and drew up an order from his seat as Judge of the Recorder's Court for Alexander Ziegler to remove his mule and wagon from the street forthwith.

Constable Lange took the writ and walked the half-mile

down to Uncle Alec's cabin to serve it. He arrived to find the old man in bed complaining of a touch of rheumatism. Uncle Alec took the court order, perused it carefully, and handed it back, explaining that he couldn't make out the judge's handwriting. Constable Lange turned the document right side up and tried reading it himself, but he couldn't make heads nor tails of Judge Skinner's scrawl either, so he hotfooted it back to the depot to have the order deciphered by the judge himself.

After fuming over the incompetence of municipal employees in general, Judge Skinner apprised the constable as to the contents of the court order and sent him back to brief Uncle Alec on his options. Uncle Alec nodded when Mr. Lange offered him the alternatives of removing his mule or else having her declared a public nuisance to be removed by whatever means the town deemed fit. Yes, he understood how Mr. Jim felt. He'd tried to get Jayrack to her feet, but everybody knew how contrary she could be. Mr. Jim knew that. He'd understand. But when the constable returned to the depot with the news that Uncle Alec had chosen to ignore the court order, Judge Skinner drew up a warrant for his arrest on a charge of willfully obstructing a public thoroughfare.

In due time Constable Lange arrived to arrest the aged miscreant, but when Uncle Alec pointed out that he couldn't come up with the ten dollars needed for bail, Mr. Lange headed back to the depot for further consultation with his honor. Agreeing that the town wouldn't want to feed an indigent prisoner for a week, Judge Skinner sent back word that Uncle Alec could remain free on his own recognizance, pending the outcome of his trial the following Saturday afternoon. About that time Jayrack got to her feet and plodded homeward, passing the very weary lawman on his way back from what he hoped would be his final trip of the day to Uncle Alec's cabin.

When word got around that Mr. Jim had sicced the law on Uncle Alec, most of the local citizens got more than a little vexed. Mr. Fate Evans tried to get the mayor to back off, but Mr. Jim was adamant. He told Mr. Fate that neither hell nor high water was going to stop him. There was too blamed much foolishness going on around Millerville as it was, and it was the mayor's duty to bring it to a screeching whoa.

The next Saturday rolled around, and at three o'clock sharp Judge Skinner convened court in the white waiting room at the depot. Those monthly judicial sessions of Mr. Jim's were always held on a Saturday, and they were naturally big events. The waiting room benches were crowded with spectators, with several others peering in through the windows. Constable Lange, in his alternate role as court bailiff, ordered all to stand as the judge entered through the front door. Then, after reciting the traditional "Oyez, oyez" from a printed card, he allowed the spectators to sit.

Judge Skinner rapped his gavel and commanded the bailiff to bring the first defendant before the bench. Mr. Lange checked his list and called for Alexander Ziegler. Getting no reply, the bailiff checked the galleries. Seeing no one that remotely resembled the defendant, the bailiff leaned over and whispered into the judge's ear. Judge Skinner grumbled and ordered the bailiff to search for Uncle Alec before the bench lost patience and handed out a contempt citation or two.

It didn't take Mr. Lange long to find Uncle Alec. He'd been waiting by the back door all along, a little bashful over the prospect of entering what had been theretofore forbidden territory. Nonetheless, he stepped forward at the bailiff's beckoning and stood politely before the dock, awaiting his fate.

Judge Skinner had just pointed an accusing finger at the defendant when Mr. Fate Evans entered the courtroom, accompanied by a well-dressed stranger. Mr. Fate pointed to Uncle Alec, and the stranger strode over, smiled, and began pumping Uncle Alec's reluctant hand. Judge Skinner took note and inquired what business, if any, the man might have before the court. The man smiled.

"I'm J. Frank Fulcher of Fulcher, Fulcher and Rountree, attorneys at law in Savannah. My card, sir."

Judge Skinner adjusted his gold-rimmed glasses and studied the card.

"Well, it looks like you're a lawyer, all right. What're you doin' in my court?"

"I've been retained as counsel for the defendant. That is, Mr. Ziegler here."

Judge Skinner arched his eyebrows at the lawyer's referring to Uncle Alec as mister, but pressed on. "You plan to defend Uncle Alec, huh? From who, I'd like to ask? Let me tell you somethin', Mr. Lawyer. Uncle Alec don't need your kind. We can handle things around here without you a-buttin' in. Now Fate, if you'll just take this big-city jackleg and ship him back to Savannah, I think we can wrap up this case in a quick hurry."

Mr. Fulcher continued: "Begging your pardon, your honor, it doesn't appear that you intend to follow due process of law in this case, certainly not as I'm accustomed to thinking of it. Let's not overlook the fact that any defendant anywhere in this nation has the constitutional guarantee of the right to legal counsel before a court of law."

"Well now, I've read the Constitution over, and I ain't never seen nothin' like that in it."

"It's there, your honor, near the end of the sixth amendment.

All we need is a sixth-grade civics text to confirm that as fact."

Judge Skinner glared at the lawyer. "Well, how about that? What in tarnation would we do without our big legal scholars, them that can cite the whole blessed Constitution, chapter and verse? If that's the way it is, then I say to hell with the Constitution. This is a free country, and we got the right to do things around here the way they ought to be done. You big lawdogs go on about due process and all that junk. Foot, if we was to wait for due process to take place around here, there soon wouldn't be nothin' left to wait for."

"Your honor, if you persist in attempting to deny this defendant the right to legal counsel, I think I should remind you that I am prepared to submit sworn affidavits to that effect to the United States Attorney's office in Savannah."

Judge Skinner paled. "Now hold your tater, Mr. Fulcher. What I meant was we don't usually do things around here the way you big-city lawyers are used to seein' them done. You see, we don't have any lawyers here in Millerville to keep us up on the latest ways to run court. To tell the truth, we don't rightly know how to proceed when a defendant has a lawyer on his side."

Mr. Fulcher smiled. "Well now, your honor, it's not really complicated. In the big courts we begin by asking the defendant for a plea, whether he wants to claim guilt or innocence."

The gallery snickered and Judge Skinner frowned in annoyance. "Yeah, I know all about that. Uncle Alec, are you guilty of lettin' that mule of yours block up the street out there last Saturday evenin'?"

For a moment it looked as if Uncle Alec was ready to own up to letting his mule sull up in the street, but Mr. Fulcher shushed him gently and whispered instructions into his ear. Uncle Alec scratched his head in bewilderment before finally replying. "Mr. Jim, this here lawyer-man told me to tell you that I ain't guilty of nothin' bad."

Judge Skinner stared at Uncle Alec in disbelief. "Well I'll be john-browned. What in the political hell do you want to stand there and tell a big story like that for, Uncle Alec? Look, I seen you myself, standin' there by that mule of yours and her a-sittin' in the street. She does it all the time. Now you can't stand there and tell me you ain't guilty because—"

"Objection. The judge presumes to serve as a witness for the prosecution. Not only does that smack of bias on his honor's part, but is highly irregular, inasmuch as his honor has not been duly sworn as a witness in the first place. Now I'm aware that in recorder's court there is no provision for a special solicitor to serve as prosecutor, nor is a jury required for handing down a verdict. However, I feel that a crime of the magnitude this one purports to be must have been witnessed by many. I'd much prefer to hear the unbiased testimony of those personages and leave the judge free to decide the merits of this strange case on the basis of such evidence."

"Well now, that's a plumb highfalutin speech. I don't have to serve as a witness, no-sir-ree-bob. You over there, Tooky Calhoun, I seen you standin' there by the well when me and Mr. Lange was tryin' to get that blasted plug to her feet. Come on up here and let me swear you in so you can tell the court just what you saw."

Tooky Calhoun rose unsteadily, wiped his mouth on his shirt sleeve, and stumbled forward to the cheers of the gallery. After a few trials, Judge Skinner finally managed to get Tooky positioned with his left hand raised and the right thrust out-ward, palm down. Then the bailiff announced that he couldn't find a Bible. Poor Tooky had to stand rigid in the swearing-in posture while Rufus Catoe ran over to the First Baptist Church to borrow one. In about five minutes the youth returned with a pocket testament, and Tooky Calhoun took the oath to tell the truth, the whole truth, and nothing but the truth, so help him God.

Judge Skinner stroked his chin, frowned, and commenced questioning the witness.

"Now Tooky, tell the court just how you seen Old Jayrack sittin' out there by the artesian well last Saturday."

"Objection. Prosecution is putting words into the witness's mouth. The witness's testimony must be rendered free of such direction."

"Now hold on, Mr. Smart-aleck. We all seen that mule sittin' out there in the street, and that's a fact."

"Your honor, I'll not gainsay the fact that a mule blocked traffic in this fair town on Saturday last. The questions before this court are, what or whose mule was involved, and did that involvement constitute a felony or a misdemeanor on the part of the owner? Neither the fact of accusation nor observations on the part of witnesses bear, perforce, any presumptions of guilt or innocence. That is for the court to decide once all the evidence has been presented."

"Well, er, Tooky, just what did you see there by the artesian well last Saturday?"

"You want me to start from when I first got to town, Jim?"

"Yes, Tooky, if it will help you to keep your story straight."

"Well, near as I can remember, me and Frank Sugg was standin' there by the artesian well a-jawin' about how the fish was a-bitin' in the river, when Lige Fails' old black sow come up and stretched out in that big mudhole where the water slops over from the well. She looked right happy a-gruntin' away there until Mr. Fate come out of his store and sicced Old Sport on her. Lord, you ought to of heard that old hog squeal when that dog latched onto her ear."

"Dammit, Tooky, you know blamed well I don't want to hear about no blamed dogs runnin' hogs. Just tell us about Old Jayrack."

"Objection. Prosecution persists in attempting to lead the witness."

Judge Skinner threw up his hands in resignation. "All right! Tooky, did you see any mules there by the artesian well last Saturday?"

"Why yeah, Jim. First I seen Coot Mixon's little old mule Ficey Ann when Coot drove her up to the well to drink. You know, I could of swore that Old Coot was already half drunk, and it wasn't even three o'clock yet. After that I saw them mules of Mr. J. B.'s when Deacon Tolbert drove by in that purty green wagon. Let's see, that black mule on the left was Old Mary, but I didn't recognize the bay mule on the right. Anybody here know the name of that bay mule who's Mary's mate?"

I was about to point out that the mule's name was Lou, when Judge Skinner broke in. "Dammit, Tooky, you know dingdonged well that I don't want to hear about every blamed mule in Ogeechee County. What about Old Jayrack?"

"Objection, objection. The prosecution is attempting to lead the witness again."

"I swanee, just what in the pluperfect hell do I have to do to get around your cotton-pickin' objections?"

"You might begin, your honor, by asking the witness if he saw a mule sitting in the street on Saturday last."

"You hear that, Tooky?"

"Yeah, Jim. What you want me to do?"

"Just answer the question, you mullet-head. Did you, or did you not, see a mule sittin' out there by the artesian well last Saturday?"

"Objection. Prosecution is badgering its own witness."

After Judge Skinner threatened to clear the courtroom, the snickering subsided somewhat, and the question was redirected.

"Yeah, Jim. I seen a mule sittin' right over yonder by the well."

All eyes followed Tooky Calhoun's finger as it pointed across the tracks in the direction of the town square, now deserted except for a small group of black women comparing their babies.

"Did you recognize the mule, Tooky?"

"Oh yeah. It was Old Jayrack, all right."

"Do you know who Jayrack belongs to, Tooky?"

"Yeah. Everybody knows she belongs to Uncle Alec Ziegler. Don't she, Uncle Alec?"

Uncle Alec was about to agree that Jayrack was indeed his property when Mr. Fulcher cautioned him to remain silent.

Satisfied that he'd made his case against Uncle Alec, Judge Skinner turned Tooky Calhoun over to Mr. Fulcher for cross-examination. After a brief pause for refreshment, the lawyer approached the prosecution's star witness and began.

"Now, Mr. Calhoun, you appear to be a man of rare perception and a witness of unimpeachable veracity, if indeed such exists."

Tooky Calhoun looked puzzled but smiled when he saw that the spectators were grinning.

"Tell me, sir, are you positive that the mule you allegedly saw sitting in the street on Saturday last was this, er, Jayrack, as I believe she's called?"

"Well, the mule I seen sure did look like Old Jayrack."

"Indeed. Now tell the court if you will, just what the mule's owner was doing all the time his alleged charge was taking her repose by the artesian well. Was he trying, by any chance, to get her to her feet?"

"Well sir, I didn't mention this before 'cause Mr. Jim didn't ask me, but, to tell the truth, I didn't see Uncle Alec nowhere near his mule."

"I see. Did you see Uncle Alec, Mr. Ziegler, that is, at all that Saturday?"

"Er, no, I didn't. It was like this. Jim Bo Wiggins got me to go over behind the blacksmith shop with him to look at some likker Fent Newsome dropped off for him to sell. Old Jim wanted me to help him sell it that night, but I had to tell him that I couldn't. I'd already promised Frank Sugg that I'd go fishin' with him. When I got back, Old Jayrack was just a-sittin' there, and Frank told me that Uncle Alec had done gone home."

"Then any information you might have connecting the defendant with the alleged crime is based upon nothing more than hearsay?"

"Huh?"

"Hearsay, secondhand report, and all that sort of thing. Are you now ready to admit that your stating under direct examination that the mule in question was the defendant's property was also based upon hearsay?"

"Well, no. I recognized the mule, and I knew the wagon too."

"There was no mention of a wagon under direct examination, but that vehicle could be brought up by the prosecution, should it so choose. We'll strike any mention of wagons for the time being and concentrate on the mule. How can you be so sure that the mule in question belonged to the defendant when you admitted under cross-examination that you didn't see the defendant near the animal, and have further testified that you have no personal knowledge that the defendant had been anywhere near the animal on the day of the alleged crime?"

"Well, the mule I seen sittin' in the street was kind of brown-lookin' and pore, and Old Jayrack looks like that."

"I see. Now tell me, Mr. Calhoun, are there any other brown-looking, skinny mules around here?"

"Yeah. Come to think of it, my Old Sooky kind of looks like that."

"Really? Then could it have been your Sooky sitting there in the street rather than Uncle Alec's Jayrack?"

"Oh no. I rode into town with Fent Newsome. Sooky was home in the lot."

"Could the mule in the street have belonged to this, er, Fent Newsome then?"

"No sir."

"And why not?"

"The mule we're talkin' about was brown, and everybody here knows that Fent Newsome's Old Pender Jane is gray."

Mr. Fulcher graciously conceded a point to the witness to the accompaniment of a chorus of guffaws from the spectators.

"One more question, Mr. Calhoun. Could it have been that the mule in question took you into her confidence? That is, she told you that she belonged to Uncle Alec Ziegler."

"Well no, she didn't. I don't think Old Jayrack can talk anyway."

"Perhaps not, but the fact that you've not heard her speak doesn't prove that she can't. Would you agree?"

"I suppose so."

"At any rate, one might hope that if she could talk she'd be circumspect enough not to peach on her owner. Mr. Calhoun, I've found you a delightful witness—clear-headed, cooperative, and pliable to a fault. Your honor, I have no further questions."

Tooky Calhoun stepped down, and Judge Skinner turned his attention once more to the defendant. "Uncle Alec, I could call other witnesses, but there ain't no need to. There ain't the slightest doubt in my mind that you're guilty as charged. You can be thankful that I'm lettin' you off light. I could of nailed you for contempt when you didn't act on my court order. Now I know you ain't got no money to pay fines with, so I'll just have to consider a term of penal servitude for you, as Mr. Fulcher and them other big lawdogs call it. Now there ain't no reason for my sendin' you over to the county jail to pull your time when there's plenty you can do right here. There's a whole bunch of trash and junk here at the depot that needs haulin' off, so I expect about five days—"

"Your honor, please, isn't this man going to be allowed to put up any kind of defense?"

Judge Skinner looked at the lawyer scornfully. "Well now, we don't generally worry about that sort of thing around here, seein' as how only the guilty ever come before this court. But if you feel like jawin' some before I pass sentence, go right ahead. Just make it snappy."

Mr. Fulcher pressed a nickel into my hand and asked me to bring him a drink. I ran over to Evans' General Store, rinsed out a pop bottle, and filled it with water from the artesian well. Mr. Fulcher thanked me and sipped the cool, sulfurous liquid while collecting his thoughts for Uncle Alec's defense. A few swallows and the lawyer was ready to begin.

"Because the defense does not intend to call any witnesses, and there seems to be little merit in having the defendant testify in his own behalf, I shall, if it pleases the court, use the time allotted in examining some of the legal and moral issues raised by this odd case. First off, I'd like to point out that there is reason to believe that no wrongful act was committed in the first place. There is no statute in the legal codes of the state of Georgia, nor any local ordinance, that specifically prohibits a mule from sitting, or even reclining, on a public thoroughfare or any other public place that it might choose. Therefore, the warrant that precipitated this hassle was very likely invalid in the first place.

"Still, I suppose one could argue with force that, even so, a mule's owner is responsible for the conduct of his animal in public places. I shall not dispute the general desirability of such a rule. Should a person own a dangerous, fractious mule, and display the brute in such a way that it does harm to persons or property, then the owner should be held responsible. If, on the other hand, the mule happens to be a harmless old plug, as the defendant's mule is alleged to be, and the owner has taken all prudent steps to curb his charge and fails, then the sympathies of the public might naturally devolve upon the beleaguered owner.

"I would like, if it pleases the court, to construct a hypothetical situation by way of illustrating the aforementioned point. Suppose that a given mule is ordinarily docile and tractable. Then, for reasons best known to itself, the mule decides to plop down smack in the middle of the town square in some mythical municipality of, say, 754 souls. The owner racks his brain figuring ways to get his stubborn charge to its feet, but to no avail. His efforts quite naturally evoke the sympathies of the standers-by, who are only too glad to offer assistance and advice, because the congestion caused by the mule tying up traffic might throw some of them late getting home so that they might have to milk and slop the hogs after dark.

"How should the good citizens proceed? First they might implore the mule to get to its feet and quit cuttin' the fool. But that didn't work with the real flesh-and-sinew mule in the current case, so there's no good reason to believe that it would work with a hypothetical mule either. Some of the more ill-tempered might try persuading the mule with a whip or a club, which seems to me a cruel, though I daresay not unusual, form of punishment. Finally the most brutal element might shoot the poor animal, and that might amount to a Sodom versus Gomorrah solution, because, as all of you are doubtless aware, dead mules are heavy and hard to tote off the road.

"Therefore, dealing with a sulled-up mule can be a problem, one that is best dealt with by keeping cool and allowing the mule to act in its own good time. I've been informed that the mule in the present case did just that. When she got tired of squatting on that sharp gravel in the town square, she got to her feet and plodded on home. Let me say, with no malice intended, that in so doing that old plug displayed, in my humble opinion, more common sense than any of us here this afternoon.

"Please don't misunderstand me. I think I can appreciate the trial it must be having to endure a mule sitting about in the streets on market days. I believe that the judge, once he returns to his everyday capacity as mayor, might wish to call the town council together to consider passing an ordinance making it at least a misdemeanor for a mule to sit, or recline, on a public thoroughfare. Such a law could not, of course, be applied in an *ex post facto* way to the present litigation. Moreover, any such ordinance should be worded so that the mule is as liable for its misdeeds as its ever-suffering master. I say that because, as all of you are doubltless aware, a mule has a mind of its own, and bends its will to that of its master only to the degree it sees fit to at any given time. Thus I say that the mule should be required to bear an equal, if not greater, responsibility for its wrongdoings than the hapless soul who purports to own and guide it.

"Now I'm aware that summoning animals to court to answer for crimes and misdemeanors might seem bizarre to many, but there are numerous precedents, some from the not-too-distant past. There was that incident during the 1920s when those folks over in eastern Tennessee tried that elephant for murder and hanged it from a railway crane. About twenty years ago there was a case in upper New York state wherein a pack of dogs was hauled into court for allegedly attacking an eight-year-old girl. Looking back further into history, we find that trying animals was commonplace. During the Middle Ages in Europe swine were frequently condemned to death for attacking children, as were dogs for killing sheep. At one time the entire field mouse population of the Rhone Valley of France was under indictment for allegedly damaging crops.

"I could cite other examples, but those few will serve for purposes of illustration. Perhaps it would be best if I had one of my firm's clerks summarize the relevant precedents in the form of a legal brief, which document I would be happy to present for the council's perusal free of charge, provided of course that the mayor wishes to act on the matter proposed."

Mr. Fulcher might have had more to say, but he never got the chance to say it. Judge Skinner gaveled him to a halt, declared the charges against Uncle Alec dropped, and cleared the courtroom, explaining that he had to get ready to meet the Augusta local. There were a few other cases on the docket, but those were postponed until the next session.

Later I learned that Mr. Fulcher was a good friend of Mr.

Fate Evans. The lawyer had arrived in Millerville the Friday before Uncle Alec's trial intending to spend Saturday drifting for white shad on the Ogeechee River. Mr. Fate and some of the townspeople had persuaded him to take the old yardman's case instead.

A few days later I ran into Uncle Alec on Back Street as he made ready to plow out the Widow Barbour's garden. While the old yardman wrestled a plow down from the wagon, Jay-rack stood nibbling away placidly at one of the widow's prized rose bushes. As I watched, the old mule nipped off a yellow rosebud, pursed her lips, and sucked it slowly into her mouth. Uncle Alec turned and scowled at her and then, spotting me, grinned.

"Son, y'all'll just have to 'scuse this here old mule. She's bound to cut the fool, and there ain't never been nothin' I could do about it."

OLD JAYRACK'S FUNERAL

AFTER Uncle Alec's trial and subsequent acquittal, life around Millerville gravitated back to its normally slow pace. Most of the citizens were content to put the incident behind them, but Mayor Skinner didn't back off one particle. He fumed and fussed around for a week and finally called the town council together, confident that he could persuade them to pass an ordinance making it illegal for a mule to sit around in the streets. The council passed no new ordinances that day, but did approve a resolution making Old Jayrack an honorary citizen of Millerville for such time as she might inhabit this green earth.

Two days later there appeared on a back page of the *Savannah Morning News* a few lines describing our latest citizen, along with a short explanation of how she had come to be so honored. Some suspected that Mr. Fate Evans had leaked the news of Jayrack's new status to the press through Lawyer Fulcher. Others laid it to Mr. Dawse Cook, the blacksmith. Whoever might have been responsible, it suited me fine. I clipped the article out and turned it in to my sixth-grade civics teacher as a current event. To this day I can't understand why Miss Gertrude Gunn awarded me a flat *D* for that day's lesson.

The news article, along with recollections of the trial, provided an excuse for much hilarity around town, so much so that Mayor Skinner chose to lie low for a while, not even venturing out to be interviewed by a reporter who drove all the way from Atlanta to write up the story of the trial and its aftermath for his paper. Well, the reporter got his story anyway, piecemeal from various citizens. The next Sunday there appeared in the magazine section of the *Atlanta Journal* a big, somewhat embellished spread, featuring a half-page picture of Uncle Alec holding Jayrack by the bridle. Uncle Alec and his mule took all the publicity in stride, carrying on as usual. In fact, Uncle Alec agreed only reluctantly to allow the reporter to take his picture, declaring that "there won't nothin' to it all."

Uncle Alec Ziegler passed away in his sleep the night of June 19, just two months after the trial. Two days later Reverend Jonas Mack preached Uncle Alec's funeral at the Simmons Branch Baptist Church. Daddy, Uncle Lester Tolbert, Mr. Fate Evans, Mr. Clay Parker, and I were among the people in attendance. Before the burial, various citizens, as was the custom in those days, stepped forward to eulogize the dead. Prince Henry Jackson pointed out that age puts a clog on all men, but that the way Uncle Alec bore up under his should serve to inspire us all. Stephen Mack said that Uncle Alec was the kind of man who, if he happened to buy a mess of fish on a Saturday evening, always took them straight home to his wife to fry.

Although Mr. Mack's testimonial was greeted with a swelling chorus of amens, it seemed odd to me, inasmuch as Uncle Alec, as far as I knew, had had no wife. I looked at Daddy questioningly, but he just smiled and offered no explanation. A few more years would pass before I could grasp fully the meaning of Mr. Mack's remarks.

Lawyer Fulcher had wanted to attend Uncle Alec's funeral, but he had been tied up in a big case. The lawyer sent his condolences in the form of an open letter to the town of Millerville. Mr. Fate Evans read the letter aloud on the spot where Jayrack had taken her now-famous repose. Just about everybody was at the reading, including Mayor Jim Skinner.

Mayor Skinner appointed himself executor of Uncle Alec's worldly estate, a title almost as long as the old man's list of properties. Unknown to most, Uncle Alec's cabin belonged to Mr. Fate Evans, who'd let the old yardman live in it rent-free for years. The few items of personal property were given to Reverend Mack, who distributed them among the poorest of his parishioners. Eventually everything was disposed of except Old Jayrack, and nobody wanted her.

About two weeks after the funeral, Ceroy Tolbert heard over the grapevine that kept the black community informed on all matters, important and trivial, that Pegleg Cleland, the itinerant mule jobber, was due in town. Rumor had it that Mayor Skinner was planning to let him have Jayrack. Pegleg Cleland bought mostly worn-out plugs for slaughter, so it looked like Millerville's newest honorary citizen might end her days in a pet-food can.

I ran to Daddy with tears in my eyes and begged him to let me keep Jayrack on our farm. Daddy didn't think much of my idea, pointing out that he was already feeding more mules than he had use for. I countered by explaining that Jayrack was too old to work and wouldn't need much to eat. I thought she would be happy cropping grass with the milch calves in the little five-acre pasture by our barn. Daddy agreed to take the old mule in only after I promised not to sneak any feed out to her. That much accomplished, I ran off in search of Ceroy.

I found my pal at home toting in stovewood. To save time, I helped by carrying a couple of armloads myself. Once we'd filled the woodbox to the brim, we skedaddled before Ceroy's mother could catch him and assign more chores. We ran every step of the two miles to Millerville; we were that anxious to save old Jayrack.

We found Mayor Skinner at the depot sorting through a stack of freight waybills. He didn't even look up when we asked him if we could take Uncle Alec's mule. He mumbled for us to take the blasted plug and get out so he could get some work done.

Old Jayrack brayed for joy when we arrived at Uncle Alec's cabin. She didn't look as if she'd enjoyed a square meal since her master's death—not that she'd been fed to the point of founder when he was alive. She was so thin we despaired that she would be able to make the journey to our place, but the old plug was tough. She made the two miles with ginger to spare.

Luckily Daddy was away when we got back. That way we were able to treat Jayrack to some oats and a few ears of corn before we turned her into the calf pasture. There were times after that when my conscience bothered me for going back on my word to Daddy, but I just couldn't seem to help sneaking out tidbits to the old mule now and then. On those handouts and the good grass of the pasture, Jayrack mended fast, so that by early autumn she looked like a different mule from the one that had eluded Pegleg Cleland's grasp.

One morning in October I went out early to drive in the calves for the morning milking. We didn't take a new calf away from its mother the way dairies do nowadays. We kept our calves and let them grow up sharing their mother's milk. That morning was the kind that made one glad to be alive and out early. The air was cool but not yet cold. The trees along the fencerow seemed in a dilemma over whether to drop their leaves or to hold them for a few more days. Light fog drifted over the spent goldenrod in the fence jambs, festooning the cobwebs draped over them with droplets of moisture so that they glittered like so many elfin tiaras. I felt the need to commune with Old Jayrack, so I put off driving in the yearlings while I ran in search of her. I found her in a far fence corner, shrouded in dew and still in death.

I've always dreaded the loss of a favorite pet, but oddly I had no tears for Jayrack. Perhaps it was because I knew that she had never really been our mule after all. She could never have belonged to anyone except Uncle Alec Ziegler, whom she'd now chosen to join.

I told Daddy and he just shrugged. "I'm sorry to hear that, Jamie. I guess, like all things must, she just came to the end of her days. I'll have C. T. Tolbert hitch up a team and drag her off to the creek swamp."

"Can't we bury her there in the pasture, Daddy?"

"I'm afraid not, son. I can't spare any hands right now to dig a hole for her. We've got to get the corn crop in before the winter rains set in."

"Would it be all right if me and Ceroy dug a grave for her?"

Daddy laughed. "Well, it's all right with me, but we can't leave her there too long. I don't see how you boys expect to do such a big job with school and all, but I'm willing to leave that up to you."

Ceroy and I started the grave that afternoon after school. Neither of us had foreseen the task involved in digging a mule-sized grave some six feet deep. Even so, we toiled until dusk and managed a hole of the required breadth some six inches deep. While we shoveled away, we planned the funeral. I thought it would be fitting for us to read a psalm or two over the grave, but Ceroy had a much better idea. He thought it would be nice if we could get Reverend Jonas Mack to preach the funeral, just like for folks.

Later I realized that my pal had been jesting, but at the time the suggestion seemed not only brilliant, but eminently practical as well. Ceroy tried to back off when I started pressuring him to take the proposal to Reverend Mack, but in the end I won out. I finally got Ceroy to agree to at least ask the parson what he thought of the idea.

The next day was Saturday, and Ceroy showed up for the grave digging with a long face. He'd been afraid to approach Reverend Mack with such a bizarre proposal and had instead talked his older brother, C. T., into seeing the preacher in exchange for a new jackknife. C. T. Tolbert, in sharp contrast to his baby brother, was a dull sort of fellow, easily led, but that time it looked like my pal had bitten off more than he could chew. Reverend Mack had flown into a perfect dudgeon over the suggestion that he preach a funeral for a lowly jarhead. He'd proceeded to bless C. T. out, and had threatened to report the youth's impertinence to his father. The upshoot of the whole affair was that Ceroy was having to lie low until his brother cooled off.

With that dismal news to ponder, we took up shovels and headed for the grave site. We arrived to find dirt flying from the pit. We'd not expected any help, so we were pleasantly surprised when two of Daddy's farmhands, Quill Robertson and Dessie Lee, climbed from the pit grinning. Quill spoke:

"Cap'n sent us to help you boys before we took off for town. I expect she's deep enough to hold that old plug now. Ceroy, who you goin' to get to handle it? I hear tell Grace's Parlour turns out a right good funeral for as cheap as forty dollars."

That prompted chuckles all around, and I was about to suggest that we get a team to drag Jayrack to the grave when C. T. showed up driving Mutt and Jeff. Old Jeff snorted and shied at the sight of a dead comrade, but at C. T.'s urging, he settled down and did his duty.

We had just finished patting the last shovelful of soil on the grave when I looked up and beheld a small party filing through the pasture gate. Daddy was in the lead, followed by Uncle Lester Tolbert, Mr. Fate Evans, Deacon Andrew Tolbert, and wonder of all wonders, Reverend Jonas Mack.

Once we'd all assembled around the grave, Reverend Mack had us make a circle and bow our heads. Then, after a moment of reverent silence by way of effecting the proper attitude toward the departed, the preacher began.

"Brethren, we are gathered in the sight of the Lord to speak a few words over this here old mule, beloved companion and loyal helpmate for all them years to Uncle Alec Ziegler, one of the most devout and upright of God's children. Now I've heard claims that mules don't have souls, and therefore there ain't no place in paradise for them. Well, let me tell you, brethren, I know the Holy Scriptures about as well as the good Lord will allow any mortal to know them, and the plain truth is there ain't one word in the Holy Book on the subject of whether or not mules, or horses, or cows, or jackasses, or any other kinds of animals have souls. So you see, brethren, the Bible don't say they do, and it don't say they don't.

"What is a soul anyway? Well, it ain't for me to know exactly. I hear tell that the Pope over there in Rome don't know exactly what a soul is, and the Archbishops don't know, and the Bishops don't know neither. Now if them high churchmen don't know exactly what a soul is, you can't expect an old country preacher like me to know. But as long as that's the way it is, I expect I'm entitled to speculate on what a soul is as much as the next fellow. So let me tell you, brethren, what I think a soul is like.

"A person's soul is kind of like what we seem to be to others, and that is what a man is apt to wind up bein'. Them's the things we have to abide in a man when he's here, and what we remember him by when he's gone. It's the good and the bad in womenfolks and men, and the Holy Scriptures say it's what the good Lord weighs out on Judgment Day.

"Now we know that folks do good, and they sin; Lord have mercy on us, for we are of flesh. Mules don't know nothin' about sinnin'; course some of them can be mighty aggravatin' at times. Take this here old mule that we just laid to rest. She could be a trial when she felt like it. You all remember that time back there in the spring when she caused Mr. Jim Skinner to get so upset."

With mention of Jayrack's part in the great court hassle, we all broke out in laughter, and Reverend Mack was forced to grin himself.

"Course, she didn't know she was doin' wrong, and anyway, this here old mule never done much wrong nohow. She spent her days a-workin' alongside her master, the way a good mule is supposed to do. She took fodder for her payment and didn't complain much. That took a lot of soul, more'n some folks I know have got. So if mules do have souls, this one's deservin' of a place on high, and that's a fact.

"Now I've speculated on it from time to time, and I reckon heaven is, in some ways, like it is down here. Of course there ain't no drinkin', or carryin' on, or cuttin' the fool up there. Little angel children most likely have dogs and cats, and maybe a few biddies, to play with, and farm folks who've done gone to their reward might be pleasured to see some cows a-grazin' in them heavenly pastures.

"Uncle Alec didn't have nobody on this earth except his old mule. I believe he's goin' to be lonely without her. I just got to believe that a just Lord, praise His name, sees to it that the righteous are reunited with them they loves, whether it's people or animals. It wouldn't surprise me none to know that Old Jayrack is up there now, pullin' Uncle Alec's little wagon through them golden streets.

"In the fullness of time, brethren, all the chosen will be gathered on that other shore. That might include mules, and it might not. If it does, there's one thing we can be sure of: when the roll is called up yonder, Old Jayrack's goin' to be there. Let us pray."

After the funeral, Daddy passed around a pitcher of lemonade. As we stood sipping the cold, tart liquid, C. T. Tolbert edged around to where Ceroy and I stood.

"I expect you boys is mighty surprised to see Reverend Mack here. Ain't you?"

I had to admit that we were, and that we were naturally curious as to why the parson had changed his mind. C. T. scratched his head, grinned, and replied. "Well, I don't know exactly why he changed his mind, but early this mornin' he come by to tell on me. He looked real mad, and I expected that Pappy was goin' to whup me, and if he done that, I was goin' to whup Ceroy. Pappy was talkin' with Cap'n when Reverend Mack come up. They all set in to arguin', and then I heard them say somethin' about doin' it for the chillun. Then they all started laughin', and we come on over here."

When I look back on the occasion, I suppose that Ceroy and I did strain propriety a bit by prevailing upon Reverend Mack to preach Old Jayrack's funeral, even if we did do it in a roundabout way. Still, I'm glad that he did, and equally glad that Daddy and Deacon Tolbert were able to talk him into changing his mind. As the parson pointed out, Jayrack had a heap of soul, certainly more than most mules, and enough, we hoped, to get her through those pearly gates.

A HORSE NAMED FOX

NO COMPENDIUM of tales about mules could be complete without at least one about a horse. The mule is, after all, half horse, and aside from that the relationships between horses and mules are so fascinating that it would be difficult to characterize fully the personality of the mule without some reference to the way the humble jarhead feels about his elegant cousin, the horse.

Horses obviously antedate mules in the history of domestication. Moreover, some breeds of horses have been treasured since time immemorial as the proper trappings of nobility, whereas the mule, with rare exception, has always been regarded as a mere beast of burden, barely a cut above its father, the lugubrious ass. Perhaps that is why mules defer to horses when the two are permitted to run together.

Aside from lording it over the mule, the horse has another fascinating trait, one rarely observed in the lowly hardtail. Some horses will literally die in the service of their masters, a thing the average mule is very reluctant to do. Romantics ascribe this property of the horse to nobility of character, whereas the more cynical think it stems from a lack of common sense. Fox, a chestnut gelding of my grandfather's, laid down his life in the service of his master. As I recall the time and circumstances, the horse had no choice. Still, I'd like to believe that had Fox known what was being asked of him, he would have paid the price gladly.

Fox was not a pedigreed animal. In fact, we knew nothing

of his ancestry, Grandfather having bought the gelding from a Mr. Henley, who'd bought the horse earlier from a band of Romany Gypsies. Because Old Fox was such a quiet, even-tempered horse, Grandfather speculated that the Gypsies who'd dealt him to Mr. Henley had stolen the animal just a few days before; that way they hadn't had time to train Fox as a trick horse to be used in their petty swindles.

To the end of his days Old Cap'n Tolbert preferred travel in a buggy. He had nothing against automobiles, as long as others drove them. When he needed to make a long trip, like over to the county seat some twenty-five miles away, one or the other of his sons was always glad to drive him. For trips to town or just riding about the countryside, the leisurely pace of a spoke-backed buggy was more to Grandfather's old-fashioned tastes.

I remember the Saturday morning Fox was delivered. Grandfather hitched him to a new buggy and drove down to Millerville to show him off. It didn't matter that folks were accustomed to seeing Mr. Henley drive Fox to town. He looked like a different horse with the Old Cap'n at the reins.

The relationships between Fox and the twenty-odd mules in Grandfather's barn lot turned out to be most remarkable. If a new mule is turned into a barn lot where the peck order is already worked out, the alien will be avoided at first. Then, as curiosity overcomes foreboding, the indigenous mules approach the stranger to feel it out. If the new mule is to find its way into the existing order, it must work its way in gradually, or else it must fight its way in. Turn a horse into the same lot, and the mules will stumble over each other to get near it. Those that manage to jostle their way in closest to the horse nuzzle it and hum contentedly. The horse, on the other hand, might show total indifference to the mules, or it might take advantage of their affections and wind up dominating them completely. Mules seem to be especially fond of mares, and I've seen a few mares who couldn't stand the overwhelming attentions of a herd of mules for long. Such animals had to be kept away from jarheads to preserve their sanity.

When Grandfather turned Fox into his barn lot, Old Suitie, a stout, iron-gray mule, was boss. On spying Fox for the first time, Suitie trotted over, thrust her neck over Fox's withers, and stood stock still. Grandfather explained that placing the head over the shoulders of another is an aggressive gesture in stallions, but a goodwill sign in mules. It was Suitie's way of telling Fox that he could be boss in her place, if that was to his liking.

The subordinate mules seemed to approve of Suitie's gesture, and Fox could have been the undisputed boss of the barn lot, if he'd wanted to. Instead, Old Fox, although granted all the prerogatives that went with leadership, took not the slightest interest in ruling. He wouldn't discipline mules trying to move up in the ranks, nor did he seem interested in how the peck order was put together in the first place.

Fox's aloofness pleased Grandfather no end. It meant that his new buggy horse could hold his own among the mules without getting involved in their petty squabbles. However, the result of Fox's intransigence was a total disruption of the social order among the mules. By the time the peck order had been sorted out once more, Suitie had been deposed as leader, and a black mule named Kit had taken her place.

I was elated to have Grandfather come into a horse like Fox. The mare he'd had before the gelding had been too high-strung for a boy my age to ride. Just about anybody could have ridden Fox, and I was allowed to ride him as often as I liked, provided, of course, he wasn't needed at Grandfather's buggy.

That summer with Fox was about the happiest of my boyhood. At the time I wouldn't have dreamed that there was sorrow on the horizon.

By the 1930s Grandfather was in semi-retirement. Freedom from the cares of managing a large plantation meant that he could devote more time to church and lodge work, and to activities such as picking mules for his neighbors. It was while selecting mules that the trouble began. Over Grandma's protests, the Old Cap'n attended a mule sale in late January of 1936, although he was suffering with a touch of grippe. He came down with pneumonia shortly after returning home.

Although Grandfather was robust for his age, it became quickly obvious that he would need all his stamina, plus a goodly measure of luck, to pull through. That was long before the days of antibiotic drugs, so little could be done for pneumonia patients other than make them as comfortable as possible and pray that they could muster the reserves of strength needed to shake the dangerous malady. Dr. Josh Barnes administered such medicines as were available, and swaddled and sweated Grandfather with mustard plasters, but to no avail. The good doctor wanted to move the patient to the county hospital or to a clinic in Savannah where a new serum was being tried on pneumonia sufferers, but Grandfather would have none of it. He said that if his time had come, he wanted to pass in the bosom of his family and near his many friends.

Just as Dr. Barnes was about to despair that the clinic would be able to part with any of the precious serum, word arrived that a supply was being dispatched on the evening express, which was due in Millerville at 12:37 that night.

Though I've never been particularly superstitious, I remain convinced that that night was cursed. Perhaps poor planning as a result of our state of anxiety was to blame. Whatever the cause, everything we attempted that wretched night seemed to go wrong. First, Dr. Barnes was called away to assist a midwife with a difficult delivery on the Clay Parker place. Then, as the time approached to meet the train, Daddy's old Ford wouldn't start. Uncle Lester's Dodge was laid up, and Dr. Barnes would need his car to rush back to Grandfather's bedside to administer the serum, once it arrived.

More out of youthful concern than for any other reason, I offered to ride Fox down to the station to get the serum. To my surprise, Daddy and Uncle Lester liked the idea, but demurred over letting me make the ride. Instead they decided to send C. T. Tolbert after the serum while I rode a mule over to the Parker place to check up on Dr. Barnes' progress. I agreed, but was naturally miffed that my elders thought I was still too much of a boy to shoulder such an important responsibility as saving Grandfather's life.

We lost no time saddling Fox and Rhodie, a gentle old plug mule the neighborhood kids liked to ride. C. T. mounted Fox, and after a short pause for instructions, urged the gelding into a gallop. I sat watching for a moment and urged my own mount onward toward the Parker place.

My teeth chattered as Rhodie's hooves rhythmically crunched the frozen surface of the public road. A cold front had pushed through the night before, and the air was so still and heavy I could have sliced it with a butcher knife. Ice sprouting from the claygalls on the ditch banks shimmered and sparkled in the moonlight that filtered in through the bare trees. An animal started in a roadside thicket and tripped away over dry leaves; a dog or a coon most likely, but my thoughts turned to tales of panthers along Big Horse Creek. Rhodie shied and murmured in her throat. I pressed her flanks, more to reassure myself than for any other reason. That seemed to calm the old mule, and I felt better too.

A long, mellow wail told me that the express was nearing the Ogeechee crossing, four miles down the line. I watched the train's headlight beam as it winked its way ever closer to Miller-ville. In a few short minutes Fox would be speeding back to Grandfather with the life-giving serum. Two short whoops meant a stop. The tone of the whistle told me that Cap'n Bob Norman, one of my boyhood heroes, was at the throttle. If anything could save Grandfather, it was Cap'n Bob and Fox.

I stopped and listened as the train ground to a halt. I could just see Mr. Jim Skinner handing C. T. the serum and imploring the youth to waste no time in getting it back to Grandfather's bedside. The train chuffed off. As it cleared the station, I saw flashes against the winter sky. I knew that Charlie Joyner, the Cap'n's black fireman, was feeding the great locomotive the coal that gave it life. I sat transfixed as I watched the cadenced glow of the engine's firebox as its butterfly doors swung open and shut to the rhythm of Old Charlie's nimble shovel. I wanted Charlie to give that huge black machine all the coal it wanted because it must have been tired from racing all the way from Savannah with Grandfather's serum.

A pair of headlamp beams brought me back from my reverie. I reined Rhodie over to let them pass. Doctor Barnes beeped as he sped by. Evidently the problem at the Parker place had been resolved, and just in the nick of time. I swung Rhodie around and prodded her into her best jog.

I arrived to find Fox by the front gate, lathered and heaving like a set of bellows. I helped C. T. walk him cool and rub him down. Before we stabled Fox for the night, I hugged him and whispered into his ear that he was the best horse there ever was. Uncle Lester came out later. He told us that Dr. Barnes had administered the serum but that it would be a few hours before we knew whether it would help.

I wish I could report that Old Cap'n Tolbert rallied and was up and around by the time young cotton was cracking the ground, but that was not to be. My Grandfather died in his sleep near dawn, January 31, 1936. The serum, like so many things born with bright promise for the betterment of mankind, had been worthless.

We let Fox rest for a week before I took him out for a canter around our calf pasture. He seemed fine on the first lap but came up heaving on the second. I walked him back to the barn, where he stood panting for almost half an hour. Two days later Swint Fuller came by. We had him examine Fox. The old horse doctor pronounced Fox windbroken, and as all know, there's no way to cure a bellowsed horse. We retired Fox to the calf pasture, where he wasted away and died that June. We buried him on the spot where he fell.

I have been riding horses and mules since I was five, but I always felt a little prouder when sitting a horse like Fox than even a good-riding mule. Horses rarely have the gumption of mules, nor do they often have a mule's special character. Still, a fine horse has style and beauty that no jarhead could ever hope to match. No wonder mules go wild over horses.

OLD ALEC

I'VE known many mules in my time, and although some were as contentious as a country judge, there was something likable in practically all. I'd be hard pressed to pick a favorite among the lot. Still, if I were pressed a little harder than real hard, I believe I would go along with Daddy's old plug, Alec.

That choice might seem a bit odd to some of the folks who knew the mule, for Alec was the very antithesis of what most expected a mule to be. He was grotesque and utterly without style, and his singular brand of contrariness became a local legend. Yet I loved that old hardtail, so much so that today I think of him more as a pet than as a mere beast of burden.

Those who remember Old Alec, and I daresay that few who knew him could ever forget him, will recall that he was a rare humpbacked, or hogbacked, mule. Typically a mule is peaked at the withers, somewhat swayed along its back, and peaked once more at the usually ample rump. In contrast, Alec's spine curved upward in the middle, somewhat like that of an anemic camel's, so that there were three peaks along his backline, the highest being in the center.

By the time I got old enough to work with mules, Alec was phlegmatic to the point of pure inertia. His best gait had never been more than an ambling jog even in his youth, and he was so gentle we kids could walk beneath his belly and even lift his hooves without any fear that he'd harm us in any way. Ceroy Tolbert and I liked to ride him double, bareback that is, to round up our milch cows. If there are any who doubt that riding a hog-backed mule without a saddle is some kind of feat, I invite them to try it. But then I suppose the question of whether or not Alec would have ridden more comfortably with a saddle was academic anyway, because I never saw the saddle that would have fitted over that crooked back.

Grandfather brought Alec to Millerville. The time was early December, 1918. The Great War had just ground to a halt; yet the price of cotton remained high. Farmers felt bullish about growing the crop, thus creating a market for new work stock. As a result, when Grandfather left for a mule sale in Chattanooga that year, he took along orders for 50 head of good-quality cotton mules.

As the Old Cap'n told it, he'd filled most of his orders when he came across this hogbacked mule in one of the auction stalls. The mule had been peering over the stall's half door when Grandfather approached, but had taken just one look before turning and facing the opposite wall. Old Cap'n Tolbert didn't take much to shamefaced mules, knowing that they were sometimes flighty and unpredictable. Nevertheless, he decided to test the mule's reactions further, so he flipped his Stetson at the animal and waved his arms. Alec, as the mule was named, didn't seem to notice. Ordinarily when a mule flunked the hat test, Grandfather moved on to the next stall. However, as Grandfather turned to leave, Alec faced him once more, and it was then that the Old Cap'n realized why the mule had caught his attention in the first place. Alec's long, sad face with its roman profile reminded him for all the world of Mr. Sam Newton, the Worshipful Master of the Millerville chapter of the Masonic Lodge.

Later Grandfather admitted that he'd bought Alec as much for the resemblance as for any other reason. Yet there is no evidence that he ever pointed out the likeness to Mr. Newton, or to anyone else outside of family and kin. Like most gentlemen of his time and ilk, the Old Cap'n indulged humor only with a few intimates, and then only in private. Chances were he thought better of running the risk of insulting such an important person and friend as the Worshipful Master.

Alec arrived in Millerville a week later in a carlot of horses and mules. He was last out of the stock-car door, and balked when Uncle Lester Tolbert attempted to lead him down a ramp to the ground. That caused Grandfather some concern about his new mule. Yet in spite of a tendency to get fractious when confronted with the extraordinary, Alec proved to be well worth his hay and oats. He didn't step out as briskly as Grandfather liked, but he was tireless and never seemed to get overheated the way some faster mules did. Ahead of a good plow hand, Alec could cover between four and five acres of cotton ground per day, a respectable turn for any mule.

It became clear early in Alec's stay on Grandfather's plantation that he was one jarhead who wouldn't take abuse from those who worked him. Mistreat some mules and they'll sull up; others will fight back, or even run away. Get mean with Alec, and he'd just cock his head sideways and start rambling, either along the rows or across them. When that happened, it was best to try to rein him up and speak soothingly, or else he'd keep walking until he found his stable.

Grandfather was dead set against field hands abusing his work stock. Deacon Andrew Tolbert told of a time when a young rowdy named Joe Henry McCrone hired on as a wage hand. The Old Cap'n tried him with Alec, and that didn't work out at all. Hardly had the pair settled in on a row before Joe Henry started cussing Alec and slapping him with the plow-lines. Alec took off for the barn lot, dragging plow and plow hand behind him. Needless to say, Joe Henry McCrone landed back on the road the same day he was hired.

Daddy returned home from France on May 9, 1919, and he and Mama were married that June. For a wedding gift Grandfather deeded them 150 acres of cleared land and threw in Alec to help work it. Thus did that old humpbacked mule become a member of my family before I came along.

If patience with mules is inherited, Grandfather couldn't have passed on much of it to his sons. Under Daddy's ownership Alec took on some bad habits, or else some of his old ones found new life. He got to where he wouldn't set foot in a rain puddle, nor would he go near any kind of hole in the ground. Moreover, I don't believe a log skidder could have dragged him across a plank bridge if there was a hole of any size in it.

Folks around home still chuckle about the trouble Mama had with Alec on the Simmons Branch bridge. One Saturday morning in the spring of 1922, Mama and my brother Frank took off for town with Alec hitched to a new spoke-backed buggy. All went well until they arrived at the old rickety bridge on the outskirts of town. Alec trotted about halfway across and stopped abruptly. Mama urged him on, but he refused to move. She even got down from the buggy and tried to lead him across, but that stubborn jarhead planted his hooves and refused to budge.

About that time Mama must have gotten right mad because she climbed back into the buggy, took the buggy whip, and started laying it onto Alec's reluctant rump. That proved to be a big mistake. First Alec tried backing up, but the more he backed, the more he backed into Mama's hot whip. Caught between Mama's wrath and a threatening knothole, the poor mule tried to escape by going sideways. In the process he made a complete U-turn in the middle of the bridge and got the buggy's rear axle lodged behind a banister.

Alec was a powerful animal. A couple of lunges, and the buggy parted in the middle. Before Mama could so much as utter whoa, Alec yanked the reins from her hands and took off for home, the front wheels of the shattered buggy clattering along behind him. Luckily for Mama, Swint Fuller happened along in his veterinary van and graciously offered her a lift home. When they arrived, they found Alec standing before the barn-lot gate, waiting, as if nothing had happened, for someone to take him out.

Daddy never stopped trying to reform Old Alec. One morning in the spring of 1928 he and a farmhand named Jake Plummer were breaking some new ground for a sweet potato patch. The soil was full of tree roots, making it tough to turn with a moldboard plow. However, Jake and Alec did well enough until they approached a small depression where a stump had burned out. Alec took a wide detour around the hole, and refused to go near it again on the second round. Jake yelled back:

"What ails this here mule, Cap'n?"

Daddy shook his head. "Hold up until I get there, Jake. The blamed old fool's smelled a snake or something."

A few shovelfuls of soil would have remedied the problem, but Daddy didn't think that way. He never compromised with a recalcitrant mule. He grabbed Alec's bit and tried to drag him through the hole, but Alec just raised his head and shied around the depression as before. The same thing happened on the next round, and the next, until my frustrated father gave up in disgust.

An even more bizarre event involving Old Alec took place

in the late 1930s, an incident that also involved me. We were barning tobacco that sultry day in July. Ceroy Tolbert and I had been assigned the task of sledding tobacco to a shed where crews strung the ripe leaf onto sticks. I don't recall which mule Ceroy had hitched to his sled, but I had Old Alec. Alec was past twenty by then, but his quirks were as strong as ever, maybe even stronger.

Just as we knocked off for dinner, a quick thunderstorm blew up, drenched the countryside, and drifted away. When we went back to work at one, dark clouds trailing a curtain of rain grumbled away to the northeast, while a full rainbow arced the sky. I hitched Alec to my sled and took off for the tobacco patch where Daddy and the priming crew were already cropping the ripe tobacco. In those days primers stacked armloads of tobacco in turn rows for the sled boys to pick up. I'd gathered about half a sled load of leaf and was looking for more when Alec balked at a rain puddle. Up ahead Daddy yelled for me to bring the damned sled on before the cropped leaf started scalding in the sun. I shouted that I couldn't get Alec to budge. With that, Daddy came rushing back with his hackles higher than a wild shoat's bristles. He grabbed Alec by the bit and turned to me.

"Son, lay that plow line on his worthless ass while I pull. I intend to get this aggravatin' sonofabitch through this mudhole if I have to fair yank his no-account neck out by the roots."

I frailed away while Daddy tugged. Finally the old plug started, but not down the turn row. Instead he veered off on a slant across the rows and didn't halt until he came to a fence. In the process he dragged Daddy and the sled through a quarter of an acre of tobacco that had been primed only twice. As if that weren't bad enough, the sled turned over, scattering the tobacco I'd gathered all over the field.

I thought Daddy was going to have a seizure. He stomped his hat into the dirt and cussed Old Alec up one side and down the other, declaring that murder was too good a fate for the worthless old plug. Naturally I thought Daddy was just blowing off steam, but when he fell silent and looked real grim-like, I began to have second thoughts. I really began to get alarmed when Daddy stalked away without so much as a by your leave to anyone.

Ceroy and I had been giggling and snickering from a safe distance away before Daddy left, but we sobered up in a quick hurry when we saw him returning with a double-barreled shotgun cradled beneath his arm. While we gaped in stunned silence, Daddy nonchalantly raised the gun and aimed it at Alec's withers.

I still believe that Daddy would have ended Old Alec's days then and there with double-aught buckshot if Deacon Tolbert hadn't stepped in. The Deacon tapped Daddy on the shoulder and spoke softly.

"Jimmy, maybe we better think this thing over. If you go ahead and shoot that mule where he's at, either we are goin' to have to take down this fence to drag him out, or else we are goin' to have to drag him back through the 'bacco patch. I know you ain't about to leave no dead mule lyin' up this close to your house."

Daddy paused, considered the alternatives, and lowered the shotgun. "Son, take that old fool out and get another mule. We've got to get this damned tobacco barned before dark."

The primers grinned, and we all murmured in relief. As had happened many times before on our farm, Deacon Tolbert's quiet wisdom prevailed and another disaster was averted. I finished the day with Alice. Most of the tobacco plants flattened by the sled recovered with time, and all in all the damage was not nearly so great as it had seemed on first appraisal.

It was no accident that Alec's ways became legendary, not only in our community but as far away as two counties over. The old mule never took the short way anywhere if a longer route could be found. The following incidents may be taken as two additional cases in point.

One morning Deacon Tolbert hitched Alec to a Jersey wagon to drive up to Scarboro Crossing. On the way, Alec refused to cross the Big Horse Creek bridge. Being a practical sort, the Deacon didn't urge the reluctant mule on. He just turned Alec down off the road and let him ford the creek below the bridge. To this day I can't fathom why that old hardtail would balk at putting his hooves into a rain puddle, yet have not the slightest qualm about wading a creek up to his belly.

Another morning I had Alec hitched to a moldboard plow, working up Mama's kitchen garden, when we turned up a bumblebee nest. I took off like a scalded cat with a swarm of angry bees buzzing at my heels. When I finally mustered the courage to look back, I beheld Alec standing where I'd left him, the angry bumblers methodically popping his leathery hide. Later Ceroy Tolbert and I counted twenty-six places on Alec's flanks where the hair had turned white, such is the virulence of a bumblebee's sting. Why, I ask, should a mule be terrified of crossing a plank bridge, yet have not the slightest regard for a nest of angry bumblebees?

The loafers who hung around Cook's blacksmith shop on Saturdays never tired of enquiring of me how Old Alec was getting on and arguing over how the mule came by his deformed back. A few thought that he might have been born that way, a doubtless correct but much too prosaic explanation for men who led generally prosaic lives. Mr. Dawse Cook thought that Alec might have strained the hump into his back doing hard labor, and that his spine had then locked up that way. Sam Catoe, who was hard to top as a yarn-spinner, agreed that Alec had been born with a hogback, but suspected that his mother might have been frightened by a camel. Mr. Clyde Tilley claimed that if one rubbed a humpbacked mule along the backbone for an hour each night with a stout corncob, the hump would gradually disappear. Daddy tried Mr. Clyde's treatment on Alec, but got no results. Mr. Clyde explained away the failure by insisting that Daddy had not rubbed hard enough.

Although Alec was nearing thirty when I went away to the army in 1942, he still worked for his keep on the farm, plowing gardens and doing other piddling chores. I met a private in the army named Ruben Jenkins, an older man from Endy, North Carolina. Ruben carried pictures of his mules and favorite saddle horse in his wallet, and that prompted me to have Mama send a photograph of Old Alec. I carried that snapshot through some of the most desperate battles of Europe, only to have it stolen, along with my wallet, a week before I was due to be mustered out.

On May 7, 1946, I caught a train for home. Mama met me at the station and explained that Daddy had wanted to come but that he had been tied up in a county commissioners' meeting. On the way home Mama mentioned that Old Alec had died two days before. He had been down with gravel, and she had wanted to call the veterinarian, but Daddy couldn't see any point in wasting a vet bill on a thirty-one-year-old mule who could barely shuffle his way to the feed trough.

I'd hardly been home an hour before my nerves began to act up. The army had briefed its prospective civilians on the problems of post-separation blues, advising sufferers to get involved with people, go to dances, pay more attention to their girl friends, and what not. What those urban-oriented head doctors had not explained was how an ex-G.I. coped with the problem in a rural setting like Ogeechee County, Georgia. I'd always found fishing relaxing during my earlier years, so I dug a few worms, whistled up Daddy's dog Spot, and took off for Big Horse Creek with a limber cane pole over my shoulder. Just walking the trails of my boyhood days eased my tensions. The bright May sun and the birds a-singing were the sort of tonic those orientation types at the separation center could never have contemplated.

As we pressed deeper into the creek swamp, I noticed that my companion was growing more and more edgy. Suddenly Old Spot growled in his throat and darted off the trail into a gallberry thicket. I heard a yelp, and two buzzards struggled upward on swishing wings. I started to part the bushes but paused. I didn't really want to see Old Alec in his present state, used up by time and toil.

I trudged on to the creek and wet my line, but my heart wasn't in fishing anymore. I threw back the few stumpknockers that had been charitable enough to bite and headed home, peeved at the world in general and with Daddy in particular. Old Alec had served us faithfully for more than twenty years. I couldn't fault Daddy for letting him die, but what I would have preferred was that Alec be buried alongside Fox and Old Jayrack. My brother and I were planning a monument for Fox's grave, and I would have liked to do the same for Old Alec. I found Daddy by the back-yard gate. I started to rebuke him, but when I saw the tears in his eyes, tears of gratitude that I was home safely from the war, the words stuck in my throat.

Mama joined us and, standing there in the twilight, I noticed that they looked weary and ever so much older than I had remembered. Then I began to suspect that war is about as hard on those who remain behind as on those who march forth to battle. My parents had worked, waited, and endured the endless anxiety over loved ones in peril, the task of keeping the nation on a wartime footing, and the endless slogans of exhortation and hate. With concerns like those, there was little wonder that my father had had no time to worry about old, worn-out mules.

Why was I so upset over Old Alec's passing? True, he had been very special to me, but so had others of our horses and mules, and I'd not had nearly so many tears for them. Perhaps it was because Alec, more than any of the others, symbolized for me the old cotton South that had spawned me and nurtured me to manhood. At that very time the vast technological and social changes generated by the war augured the demise of all Alecs and the way of life they supported. Thus I suspect that my tears were being shed not so much for that contrary old plug as for the ways that were passing—ways that would not return in my time, or in anyone else's.

EPILOGUE

MUCH has changed in the Upper Plain since my boyhood days, and its people for the most part have moved with the times they've wrought. Today, mules and farm hands are about gone, along with dusty roads, tenant shacks, and Saturday afternoons in town. In their place are concrete ribbons crowding the small towns, empty houses and lonely chimneys, and broad green fields tended by muttering farm tractors. In my youth farmers talked about the weather, cotton, mules, and how to make ends meet. Nowdays they talk about credit and cash crop allotments, six-row tractors, and commodity futures. Many of the younger folks have never seen a mule, nor have many ever met a tenant farmer. Mostly they are alert to the blare of the noon whistle, as I once was to the peal of the dinner bell.

Most of the folks I knew are gone now, but Daddy dwells on in the old big house I call home, and though he farms no more, he remains attuned to the ways of the land. When I can find the time, I like to journey down to the Upper Plain to visit with him and reminisce about the days when we had to step lively to wrest more than a decent starvation from the reluctant earth. It was man and mule in those days, both damp with the sweat of honest toil—the mule expecting only his daily hay and oats; the man hoping that come autumn he could brag to the neighbors rather than make up excuses for the man at the bank.

In the spring Daddy and I check up on the local farmers to see if they do as good a job planting as we did with our mule-drawn gear. In the summer we fret over heat waves, hailstorms, and drought. In the autumn we breathe a sigh of relief that we've pulled another crop through, even though it isn't our own.

Just about any time of the year, we're likely to pay a visit to the old Baptist graveyard. Rural and small-town folks in the South still hold clean-up and renewal days at local cemeteries. The congregation gathers on a Saturday to hoe out weeds, till unused plots, and freshen up the graves of loved ones. I'd helped out one bright day in October a year or two back. Afterwards Daddy and I browsed about, seeking the graves of folks we'd known in years past.

The Baptist cemetery at Millerville is an old-fashioned grave-yard, the kind, with its moss-draped cedars and weathered headstones, that many would not care to pass near on a moonless night. Yet I've never had any qualms about going there during either daylight or dark. Perhaps that is because I still feel close to some of the departed who helped shape my life, people like Mayor Jim Skinner and Deacon Josh Wiggins, who rest on opposite sides of a huge holly tree. Near them we found the grave of Cap'n Bob Norman, railway engineer. I'll never forget the tunes Cap'n Bob blasted out as he throttled the evening express through town. Over in the "pore folks" section we found the graves of Fent Newsome, bootlegger; Sam Catoe, yarn-spinner; Tooky Calhoun, the town clown, and Mr. Clyde Tilley.

Finally we arrived at the plots of the Parkers and the Tolberts, my ancestors and kin. After placing flowers on Mama's grave and the grave of Uncle Lester, we stopped at the head of our family plot before a large double monument of white marble, the tomb of my grandparents, Molly Parker Tolbert and James Brantley Tolbert II—the Old Cap'n. I counted up and made Grandma out to be ninety-one at her passing. Daddy smiled and allowed that the Parkers had always been a hardy bunch.

The grave slab was encrusted with lichens which partly obscured a short eulogy composed by Grandfather's brothers in the Masonic Lodge. I rubbed away the growth and read: "To J. B., from those who knew him in the fullness of his powers, a candid, solid man who drank deeply from life's cup, a man who regarded each boy as a son, and who found delight in every little girl, a born leader, a tiller of the soil, and a shrewd judge of mules."

GLOSSARY

BAG OUT   to run away suddenly without warning.

BAMBOO BRIER   the greenbrier vine, *Smilax*.

BIDDY   a chick in the South; a hen farther north.

BOTTOM   stamina and endurance.

BOW-UP   to challenge, usually with the intent to intimidate.

BUNCH COTTON   to hoe out bunches of grass.

BUTT-HEADED   hornless or polled.

CAT SQUIRREL   the gray squirrel, *Sciurus carolinensis*.

CORNBUCK   rustic corn beer.

COWBELL FROG   a small green treefrog, *Hyla cinerea*.

DOG FENNEL   a rank-growing, autumn-blooming weed of Southern roadsides.

DOWN ON THE LIFT   starved to the point of having to be lifted to a standing position.

FLAT-MOUTH   aged mule whose teeth cups have worn down flat.

FRAIL   to strike repeatedly; might be a corruption of flail.

GALLERNIPPER   a slurring of gallonnipper, a large, blood-thirsty mosquito.

GLANDERS   a progressively debilitating and highly contagious respiratory ailment of horses and mules.

GRASSHOPPER PLOW   a light, single-stock plow with the handles set well forward on the stock.

JERSEY WAGON   a one-horse wagon.

JIZZYWIT   the common katydid.

LIGHT BREAD   store-boughten white loaf bread.

NOSE TWITCH   a leather thong on the end of a small pole used for restraining mules. The thong was tightened around the end of the nose.

ONE-HORSE FARM   sixty acres or less. About fifty acres were reckoned as one plow on a larger farm.

OWLHEAD REVOLVER   a cheap "Saturday Night Special" of yesteryear; had an owl's-head logo on the frame.

PECKERWOOD SAWMILL   a small, portable sawmill.

PETE TURKEY   an expression denoting triviality.

PERISHED OUT   starved.

PLUG   a mule or horse of poor quality, usually aged.

SCOPE OF WOODS   a small woodland, perhaps a corruption of copse.

SIDE COTTON   to plow cotton with a broad, flat sweep.

STUMPKNOCKER   a small sunfish of Southern streams.

SULL UP   to quit, become virtually inert, more often applied to oxen than to mules.

THROW BEDS   to turn furrows to a row.

TURKLE   some Southern people call turtles turkles.

TY-TY   a locally distributed evergreen shrub or small tree, *Cliftonia monophylla.*